Tipping r [illegible]

CW01649562

The figu [illegible] ge of the bill or in [illegible] p for the service de [illegible] dditional gratuities [illegible] lso customary to [illegible] change.

Obviously [illegible], and the correct amount to [illegible] varies enormously with category of hotel or restaurant, size of city and so on. The sums we suggest represent normal tips for average middle-grade establishments in big cities.

	Holland	**Belgium**
HOTEL		
Service charge, bill	incl.	incl.
Porter, per bag	*f* 1–2	30 F
Bellboy, errand	*f* 2–5	40 F
Maid	optional	20–50 F
Doorman, hails cab	*f* 1–2	20–50 F
RESTAURANT		
Service charge, bill	incl.	incl.
Waiter	optional	optional
Hat check	*f* 1–2	50 F
Lavatory attendant	50 cents	10 F
Canal-boat guide	optional	–
Taxi driver	optional	optional
Tourist guide	5–10%	10%
Barber/Women's hairdresser	incl.	10–15%
Cinema/Theater usher	50 cents–*f* 1	20 F

BERLITZ PHRASE BOOKS

World's bestselling phrase books feature not only expressions and vocabulary you'll need, but also travel tips, useful facts and pronunciation throughout. The handiest and most readable conversation aid available.

Arabic
Chinese
Danish
Dutch
European (14 languages)
European Menu Reader
Finnish
French
German
Greek
Hebrew
Hungarian
Italian
Japanese
Norwegian
Polish
Portuguese
Russian
Serbo-Croatian
Spanish
Latin-American Spanish
Swahili
Swedish
Turkish

BERLITZ CASSETTEPAKS

The above-mentioned titles are also available combined with a cassette to help you improve your accent. A helpful 32-page script is included containing the complete text of the dual language hi-fi recording.

BERLITZ®

DUTCH
FOR TRAVELLERS

By the staff of Berlitz Guides

Copyright © 1972, 1980 by Berlitz Guides, a division of Macmillan S.A.

All rights reserved. No part of this book may be reproduced or transmitted in any form or by any means, electronic or mechanical, including photocopying, recording or by any information storage and retrieval system, without permission in writing from the Publisher.

Library of Congress Catalog Card Number: 72-76280

Revised edition
9th printing 1986

Printed in Hungary

Berlitz Trademark Reg. U.S. Patent Office
and other countries—Marca Registrada

Berlitz Guides
Avenue d'Ouchy 61
1000 Lausanne 6, Switzerland

Preface

In preparing this complete revision of *Dutch for Travellers*, we took into consideration a wealth of suggestions and criticisms received from phrase book readers around the world. As a result, this edition features:

- all the phrases and vocabulary you will need on your trip
- a wide variety of tourist and travel facts, tips and useful information
- a complete phonetic transcription throughout indicating the pronunciation of all the words and phrases
- a logical system of presentation so that you can find the right phrase for the immediate situation
- special sections showing the replies your listener might give to you. Just hand him the book and let him point to the appropriate phrase. This is especially practical in certain difficult situations (doctor, car mechanic, etc.)
- quick reference through colour coding. The major features of the contents are on the back cover and a complete index is provided on pages 190–191
- tipping recommendations and a comprehensive reference section in the back of the book

These are just a few of the practical advantages. In addition, the book will prove a valuable introduction to life in Holland as well as help you should you be travelling to the northern part of Belgium where approximately 5 million people speak a version of Dutch called Flemish. Life styles and patterns vary, however, between Holland and Belgium and thus the observations included on the Dutch way of life are not necessarily reflective of the Belgian scene.

There is a comprehensive section on eating out, with translations and explanations for virtually anything likely to be found on a Dutch menu. Belgian (Flemish) dishes have also been included. There is a complete shopping guide that will enable you to obtain virtually anything you could possibly want. Trouble with the car? Turn to the mechanic's manual with its dual-language instructions. Feeling ill? Our medical section provides the surest communication possible between you and the doctor.

To make the most of *Dutch for Travellers*, we suggest that you start with the "Guide to Pronunciation". Then go on to "Some Basic Expressions". This not only gives you a minimum vocabulary but also helps you to learn to pronounce the language.

We are particularly grateful to Mrs. T.E. Anderson for her help in the preparation of this book and to Dr. T.J.A. Bennett who devised the phonetic transcription. We also wish to thank the Netherlands National Tourist Office for its assistance.

We shall be very pleased to receive any comments, criticisms and suggestions that you think may help us in preparing future editions.

Thank you. And have a good trip.

Throughout this book, the symbols illustrated here indicate small sections where phrases have been compiled of what your foreign listener might like to say to *you*. If you don't understand him, give him the book and let him point to the phrase in his language. The English translation is just beside it.

Basic grammar

Dutch is a Germanic language spoken throughout Holland and, under the name of Flemish, by about 5 million Belgians. The following concise outline of some essential features of Dutch grammar will be of help to you in understanding and speaking the language.

Articles

Dutch nouns are either common gender (originally separate masculine and feminine) or neuter.

1) **Definite article (the)**
The definite article in Dutch is either **de** or **het. De** is used with roughly two thirds of all common-gender singular nouns as well as with all plural nouns, while **het** is mainly used with neuter singular nouns and all diminutives:

de straat	the street	**het huis**	the house	**het katje**	the kitten

2) **Indefinite article (a; an)**
The indefinite article is **een** for both genders, always unstressed and pronounced like *an* in the English word "another". As in English there is no plural. When it bears accent marks **(één)** it means "one" and is pronounced rather like the vowel in "lane", but a pure vowel, not a diphthong.

een man	a man	**een vrouw**	a woman	**een kind**	a child
mannen	men	**vrouwen**	women	**kinderen**	children

Plural

The most common sign of the plural in Dutch is an **-en** ending:

krant	newspaper	**woord**	word	**dag**	day
kranten	newspapers	**woorden**	words	**dagen**	days

a) In nouns with a double vowel, one vowel is dropped when **-en** is added:

uur	hour	**boot**	boat	**jaar**	year
uren	hours	**boten**	boats	**jaren**	years

b) most nouns ending in **-s** or **-f** change this letter into **-z** and **-v,** when **-en** is added:

prijs	the price	**brief**	letter
prijzen	prices	**brieven**	letters

Another common plural ending in Dutch is **-s.** Nouns ending in an unstressed **-el, -em, -en, -aar** as well as **-je** (diminutives) take an **-s** in the plural:

tafel/ tafels	table(s)	**winnaar/ winnaars**	winner(s)
deken/ dekens	blanket(s)	**kwartje/ kwartjes**	25-cent piece(s)

Some exceptions:

stad/steden	town(s)	**auto/auto's**	car(s)
schip/schepen	ship(s)	**paraplu/ paraplu's**	umbrella(s)
kind/kinderen	child(ren)		
ei/eieren	egg(s)	**foto/foto's**	photo(s)
		musicus/musici	musician(s)

Adjectives

When the adjective stands immediately before the noun, it usually takes the ending **-e**:

de jonge vrouw	the young woman
een prettige reis	a pleasant trip
aardige mensen	nice people

However, no ending is added to the adjective in the following cases:

1) When the adjective follows the noun:

De stad is groot.	The city is big.
De zon is heet.	The sun is hot.

2) When the noun is neuter singular and preceded by **een** (a/an), or when the words **elk/ieder** (each), **veel** (much), **zulk** (such) and **geen** (no) precede the adjective:

een wit huis	a white house
elk goed boek	each good book
zulk mooi weer	such good weather
geen warm water	no hot water

Demonstrative adjectives (this/that):

this	**deze**	(with nouns of common gender)
	dit	(with nouns of neuter gender)
that	**die**	(with nouns of common gender)
	dat	(with nouns of neuter gender)
these	**deze**	(with all plural nouns)
those	**die**	(with all plural nouns)

Deze stad is groot.	This city is big.
Dat huis is wit.	That house is white.

Personal pronouns

Subject		Object	
I	**ik**	me	**mij**
you	**jij** or **je** (fam.)*	you	**jou** or **je** (fam.)*
you	**u** (pol.)**	you	**u** (pol.)**
he	**hij**	him	**hem**
she	**zij**	her	**haar**
it	**het**	it	**het**
we	**wij**	us	**ons**
you	**jullie** (fam.)*	you	**jullie** (fam.)*
they	**zij** or **ze**	them	**hen**

* The familiar **jij** or **je** (singular) and **jullie** (plural) and their associated forms are used only when talking to familiars, close friends and children.

** When addressing people you don't know well, use **u** (and its associated form **uw**) in both singular and plural.

GRAMMAR

Possessive adjectives

my	**mijn**
your	**jouw** (fam.)*
your	**uw** (pol.)**
his	**zijn**
her	**haar**
its	**zijn**
our	**ons** (with singular neuter nouns)
	onze (with singular and plural nouns of common gender)
your	**jullie** (fam.)*
their	**hun**

Verbs

First a few handy irregular verbs. If you learn only these, or even only the "I" and polite "you" forms of them, you'll have made a useful start.

1) The indispensible verbs **hebben** (to have) and **zijn** (to be) in the present:

I have	**ik heb**	I am	**ik ben**
you have	**jij hebt***	you are	**jij bent***
you have	**u hebt****	you are	**u bent***
he/she/it has	**hij/zij/het heeft**	he/she/it is	**hij/zij/het is**
we have	**wij hebben**	we are	**wij zijn**
you have	**jullie hebben***	you are	**jullie zijn***
they have	**zij hebben**	they are	**zij zijn**

2) Some more useful irregular verbs (in the present):

Infinitive		**willen** (to want)	**kunnen** (can)	**gaan** (to go)	**doen** (to do)	**weten** (to know)
I	**ik**	**wil**	**kan**	**ga**	**doe**	**weet**
you	**jij***	**wilt**	**kunt**	**gaat**	**doet**	**weet**
you	**u****	**wilt**	**kunt**	**gaat**	**doet**	**weet**
he	**hij**	**wil**	**kan**	**gaat**	**doet**	**weet**
she	**zij**	**wil**	**kan**	**gaat**	**doet**	**weet**
it	**het**	**wil**	**kan**	**gaat**	**doet**	**weet**
we	**wij**	**willen**	**kunnen**	**gaan**	**doen**	**weten**
you	**jullie***	**willen**	**kunnen**	**gaan**	**doen**	**weten**
they	**zij**	**willen**	**kunnen**	**gaan**	**doen**	**weten**

3) Infinitive and verb stem:

In Dutch verbs, the infinitive generally ends in **-en**: **noemen** (to name).
As the verb stem is usually the base for forming tenses, you need to know how to obtain it. The general rule is: the infinitive less **-en**:

infinitive: **noemen** stem: **noem**

4) Present and past tenses:

First find the stem of the verb (see under 3 above).
Then add the appropriate endings, where applicable, according to the models given below for present and past tenses.

Note: in forming the past tense, the **-de/-den** endings shown in our example are added after most verb stems. However if the stem ends in **p**, **t**, **k**, **f**, **s**, or **ch**, add **-te/-ten** instead.

Present tense		Past tense	
ik noem	I name	**ik noemde**	I named
jij noemt*	you name	**jij noemde***	you named
u noemt**	you name	**u noemde****	you named
hij/zij/het noemt	he/she/it names	**hij/zij/het noemde**	he/she/it named
wij noemen	we name	**wij noemden**	we named
jullie noemen*	you name	**jullie noemden***	you named
zij noemen	they name	**zij noemden**	they named

5) Past perfect (e.g.: "I have built"):

This tense is generally formed, as in English, by the verb "to have" **(hebben)** (see page 10) + the past participle.

To form the past participle, start with the verb stem, and add **ge-** to the front of it and **-d** or **-t** to the end:

*/** See footnote, page 9

infinitive:	**bouwen** (to build)
verb stem:	**bouw**
past participle:	**gebouwd**

The past participle must be placed *after* the object of the sentence:

Ik heb een huis gebouwd.	I have built a house.

Note: Verbs prefixed by **be-**, **er-**, **her-**, **ont-** and **ver-** do not take **ge-** in the past participle.

Instead of **hebben**, the verb **zijn** (to be) is used with verbs expressing motion (if the destination is specified or implied) or a change of state:

Wij zijn naar Parijs gevlogen.	We have flown to Paris.
Hij is rijk geworden.	He has become rich.

Negatives

To put a verb into the negative, place **niet** (not) after the verb, or after the direct object if there is one:

Ik rook.	I smoke.	**Ik heb de kaartjes.**	I have the tickets.
Ik rook niet.	I don't smoke.	**Ik heb de kaartjes niet.**	I don't have the tickets.

Questions

In Dutch, questions are formed by placing the subject after the verb:

Hij reist.	He travels.	**Ik betaal.**	I pay.
Reist hij?	Does he travel?	**Betaal ik?**	Do I pay?

Questions are also introduced by the following **interrogative pronouns:**

Wie (who)	Who says so?	**Wie zegt dat?**
	Whose house is that?	**Van wie is dat huis?**
Wat (what)	What does he do?	**Wat doet hij?**
Waar (where)	Where is the hotel?	**Waar is het hotel?**
Hoe (how)	How are you?	**Hoe gaat het met u?**

Guide to pronunciation

This and the following chapter are intended to make you familiar with the phonetic transcription we have devised, which is based on Standard British pronunciation, and to help you get used to the sounds of Dutch.

As a minimum vocabulary for your trip, we've selected a number of basic words and phrases under the title "Some basic expressions" (pages 17–21).

An outline of the spelling and sounds of Dutch

The bold letters in the transcriptions should be read with more stress than the others. In the more unusual diphthongs, we print the weaker element in a raised position, e.g. **oa**^{ee} means that the **oa** element is the more prominent sound in the diphthong and the **ee** sound is short and fleeting.

The imitated pronunciation should be read as if it were English except for any special rules set out below. Of course, the sounds of any two languages are never exactly the same; but if you follow carefully the indications supplied here, you'll have no difficulty in reading our transcriptions in such a way as to make yourself understood.

Consonants

Letter	Approximate pronunciation	Symbol	Example	
f, h, k, l, m, n, p, q, t, y, z	as in English			
b	as in English but, when at the end of a word, like **p** in cup	b p	**ben** **heb**	behn hehp
c	1) before a consonant and **a, o, u,** like **k** in **keen**	k	**inclusief**	inklew**seef**
	2) before **e** and **i**, always like **s** in **sit**	s	**ceintuur**	sehn**tewr**

ch	1) generally like **ch** in Scottish lo**ch**	kh	**nacht**	nah**kh**t
	2) in words of French origin like **sh** in **sh**ut	sh	**cheque**	shehk
chtj	like Dutch **ch** followed by Dutch **j**	khy	**nichtje**	**nikh**yer
d	as in English, but, when at the end of a word, like **t** in hi**t**	d t	**doe** **avond**	doo aavont
g	1) generally like **ch** in Scottish lo**ch**, but often slightly softer and voiced	gh	**zagen**	**zaa**ghern*
	2) in a few words of French origin, like **s** in plea**s**ure	zh	**genie**	zher**nee**
	3) like **ch** in Scottish lo**ch** when at the end of a word (and quite often at the beginning)	kh	**deeg**	daykh
j	1) like **y** in **y**es	y	**ja**	yaa
	2) in certain words borrowed from French, like **s** in lei**s**ure	zh	**lits-jumeaux**	lee-zhew**mo**ᵒʷ
ng	**ng** is pronounced as in English si**ng**	ng	**toagang**	**too**ghang
nj	like **ñ** in Spanish se**ñ**or or like **ni** in o**ni**on	ñ	**oranje**	oa**rah**ñer
r	always trilled, either in the front or the back of the mouth	r	**warm**	ʋahrm
s	like **s** in **s**it or **ss** in pa**ss**	s or ss	**ross**	roass
sj, stj	like **sh** in **sh**ut	sh	**meisje**	**maiy**sher
sch	like **s** followed by a Dutch **ch**	skh	**schrijven**	**skhraiy**vern
th	like **t** in **t**ea	t	**thee**	tay
tj	like **ty** in hi**t y**ou	ty	**katje**	**kah**tyer
v	pronounced basically as in English, but is often harder and not voiced, so that, to an English or American ear,	v	**hoeveel** **van**	hou**vayl** van

* The final **n** of a word is not usually heard during a fast conversation; it is heard, however, when words are spoken slowly.

	it sounds more like **f**, especially at the beginning or end of a word			
w	quite like English **v**, but with the bottom lip raised a little higher	V̶	**water**	**V̶aa**terr
x	always like **ks** in knac**ks**	ks	**taxi**	**tahk**see

Vowels

Dutch vowels are long when at the end of a word, or when followed by a single consonant followed by a vowel, or when written double.

a	1) when short, between **a** in cat and **u** in cut	ah	**kat**	kaht
	2) when long, like **a** in cart	aa	**vader**	**vaa**derr
e	1) when short, like **e** in bed	eh	**bed**	beht
	2) when long, like **a** in late, but a pure vowel, not a diphthong	ay	**zee**	zay
	3) in unstressed syllables, like **er** in other	er*	**zitten**	**zit**tern
eu	approximately like **ur** in **fur**, said with rounded lips and with no **r** round	ur*	**deur**	durr
i	1) when short, like **i** in bit	i	**kind**	kint
	2) when long (also spelt **ie**), like **ee** in bee	ee	**bier**	beer
	3) sometimes, in unstressed syllables, like **er** in other	er*	**monnik**	**mon**nerk
ij	sometimes, in unstressed syllables, like **er** in other; see also under "Diphthongs"	er*	**lelijk**	**lay**lerk
o	1) when short, like a very short version of **aw** in la**w**n	o	**pot**	pot
	2) when long, something like **oa** in r**oa**d, but a pure vowel, with rounded lips	oa	**boot**	boat
oe	(long) like **oo** in m**oo**n and well rounded	oo	**hoe**	hoo

* The **r** should not be pronounced when reading this transcription.

PRONUNCIATION

u	1) when short, something like **ur** in **hurt**, but with rounded lips 2) when long, like **u** in French s**u**r or **ü** in German f**ü**r; say **ee**, and without moving your tongue, round your lips.	ur* ew	**bus** **nu**	burss new

Diphthongs

ai	like **igh** in s**igh**	igh	**ai**	igh
ei, ij	between **a** in l**a**te and **igh** in s**igh**	aiy	**reis**	raiyss
au, ou	Dutch short **o** followed by a weak short **u**-sound; can sound very much like **ow** in n**ow**	o^{ow}	**koud**	ko^{ow}t
aai	like **a** in c**a**rt followed by a short **ee** sound	aa^{ee}	**draai**	draa^{ee}
eeuw	like **a** in l**a**te (but a pure vowel), followed by a short **oo** sound	ay^{oo}	**leeuw**	lay^{oo}
ieuw	like **ee** in fr**ee**, followed by a short **oo** sound	ee^{oo}	**nieuw**	nee^{oo}
ooi	like **oa** in wr**o**te (but a pure vowel) followed by a short **ee** sound	oa^{ee}	**nooit**	noa^{ee}t
oei	like **oo** in s**oo**n, followed by a short **ee** sound	oo^{ee}	**roeit**	roo^{ee}t
ui	like **ear** in l**ear**n followed by a short Dutch **u** sound, as described in **u** 2)	ur^{ew}*	**huis**	hur^{ew}ss
uw	like the sound described for **u** 2), followed by a weak **oo** sound	ew^{oo}	**duw**	dew^{oo}

* The **r** should not be pronounced when reading this transcription.

Note: When two consonants stand next to each other, one will often influence the other even if it is not in the same word, e.g. *ziens* is pronounced *zeenss,* but in the phrase *tot ziens,* it is pronounced *seenss* under the influence of the t before it.

Some basic expressions

Yes.	**Ja.**	yaa
No.	**Nee.**	nay
Please.	**Alstublieft.***	ahlstew**bleeft**
Thank you.	**Dank u.**	dahnk ew
Thank you very much.	**Hartelijk dank.**	**hahr**terlerk dahnk
That's all right.	**Niets te danken.**	neets ter **dahn**ker

Greetings

Good morning.	**Goedemorgen.**	ghooder**mor**gher
Good afternoon.	**Goedemiddag.**	ghooder**mid**dahgh
Good evening.	**Goedenavond.**	ghooder**aa**vont
Good night.	**Goedenacht.**	ghooder**nahkht**
Good-bye.	**Tot ziens.**	tot seenss
See you later.	**Tot straks.**	tot strahks
This is Mr ...	**Dit is Mijnheer ...**	dit iss mer**nayr**
This is Mrs ...	**Dit is Mevrouw ...**	dit iss mer**vro**^{ow}
This is Miss ...	**Dit is Juffrouw ...**	dit iss **yur**fro^{ow}
I'm very pleased to meet you.	**Aangenaam kennis te maken.**	**aan**ghernaam **keh**niss ter maakern
How are you?	**Hoe gaat het?**	hoo ghaat heht
Very well, thank you.	**Heel goed, dank u.**	hayl ghoot dahnk ew
And you?	**En u?**	ehn ew
Fine.	**Uitstekend.**	ur^{ew}t**stay**kernt
Excuse me.	**Neemt u me niet kwalijk.**	naymt ew mer neet **kʋaa**lerk

* In Dutch, *alstublieft* is a courtesy word often added to the end of a sentence. It has no real English equivalent.

Questions

Where?	**Waar?**	∀aar
Where is ...?	**Waar is ...?**	∀aar iss
Where are ...?	**Waar zijn ...?**	∀aar zaiyn
When?	**Wanneer?**	∀ah**nayr**
What?	**Wat?**	∀aht
How?	**Hoe?**	hoo
How much?	**Hoeveel?**	hoo**vayl**
How many?	**Hoeveel?**	hoo**vayl**
Who?	**Wie?**	∀ee
Why?	**Waarom?**	∀**aa**rom
Which?	**Welk/Welke?**	∀ehlk/∀**ehl**ker
What do you call this?	**Hoe noemt u dit?**	hoo noomt ew dit
What do you call that?	**Hoe noemt u dat?**	hoo noomt ew daht
What does this mean?	**Wat betekent dit?**	∀aht ber**tay**kernt dit
What does that mean?	**Wat betekent dat?**	∀aht ber**tay**kernt daht

Do you speak...?

Do you speak English?	**Spreekt u Engels?**	spraykt ew **ehng**erlss
Do you speak German?	**Spreekt u Duits?**	spraykt ew dur^{ew}ts
Do you speak French?	**Spreekt u Frans?**	spraykt ew frahnss
Do you speak Spanish?	**Spreekt u Spaans?**	spraykt ew spaanss
Do you speak Italian?	**Spreekt u Italiaans?**	spraykt ew itahli**aanss**
Could you speak more slowly, please?	**Kunt u wat langzamer spreken, alstublieft?**	kurnt ew ∀aht **lahng**zaamerr **spray**kern ahlstew**bleeft**
Please point to the phrase in the book.	**Wijs me de zin aan in het boek, alstublieft.**	∀aiyss mer der zin aan in heht book ahlstew**bleeft**
Just a minute. I'll see if I can find it in this book.	**Een ogenblik. Ik zal proberen het in dit boek op te zoeken.**	ayn **oa**gherblik. ik zahl proa**bay**rern heht in dit book op ter **zoo**kern

I understand.	**Ik begrijp het.**	ik ber**ghraiyp** heht
I don't understand.	**Ik begrijp het niet.**	ik ber**ghaiyp** heht neet

Can . . . ?

Can I have . . . ?	**Mag ik . . . hebben?**	mahkh ik . . . **heh**bern
Can we have . . . ?	**Mogen wij . . . hebben?**	moaghern ʋaiy . . . **heh**bern
Can you show me . . . ?	**Kunt u me . . . tonen?**	kurnt ew mer . . . **toa**nern
Can you tell me . . . ?	**Kunt u mij zeggen . . . ?**	kurnt ew maiy **zeh**ghern
Can you help me, please?	**Kunt u mij helpen, alstublieft?**	kurnt ew maiy **hehl**pern ahlstew**bleeft**

Wanting

I'd like . . .	**Ik wil graag . . . hebben.**	ik wil ghraakh . . . **heh**bern
We'd like . . .	**Wij willen graag . . . hebben.**	ʋaiy **ʋ**illern ghraakh . . . **heh**bern
Please give me . . .	**Geeft u me . . ., alstublieft.**	ghayft ew mer . . . ahlstew**bleeft**
Give it to me, please.	**Geeft u het me, alstublieft.**	ghayft ew heht mer ahlstew**bleeft**
Please bring me . . .	**Brengt u me . . . alstublieft.**	brehngt ew mer . . . ahlstew**bleeft**
Bring it to me, please.	**Brengt u het me, alstublieft.**	brehngt ew heht mer ahlstew**bleeft**
I'm hungry.	**Ik heb honger.**	ik hehp **hong**err
I'm thirsty.	**Ik heb dorst.**	ik hehp dorst
I'm tired.	**Ik ben moe.**	ik behn moo
I'm lost.	**Ik ben verdwaald.**	ik behn verr**dʋaalt**
It's important.	**Het is belangrijk.**	heht iss ber**lahng**raiyk
It's urgent.	**Het is dringend.**	heht iss **dring**ernt
Hurry up!	**Vlug!**	vlurkh

It is/There is...

It is/It's...	**Het is...**	heht iss
Is it...?	**Is het...?**	iss heht
It isn't...	**Het is niet...**	heht iss neet
There is/There are...	**Er is/Er zijn...**	ehr iss/ehr zaiyn
Is there/Are there...?	**Is er/Zijn er...?**	iss ehr/zaiyn ehr
There isn't any/There aren't any...	**Er is geen/Er zijn geen...**	ehr iss ghayn/ehr zaiyn ghayn
There isn't any/There aren't any.	**Er is er geen/Er zijn er geen.**	ehr iss ehr ghayn/ehr zaiyn ehr ghayn

A few common words

big/small	**groot/klein**	ghroat/klaiyn
quick/slow	**snel/langzaam**	snehl/**lahng**zaam
early/late	**vroeg/laat**	vrookh/laat
cheap/expensive	**goedkoop/duur**	**ghoot**koap/dewr
near/far	**dichtbij/ver**	dikht**bai**/vehr
hot/cold	**warm/koud**	∀ahrm/ko^{ow}t
full/empty	**vol/leeg**	vol/laykh
easy/difficult	**gemakkelijk/ moeilijk**	gher**mah**kerlerk/**moo^{ee}**lerk
heavy/light	**zwaar/licht**	z∀aar/likht
open/shut	**open/dicht**	**oa**pern/dikht
right/wrong	**juist/verkeerd**	yur^{ew}st/verr**kayrt**
old/new	**oud/nieuw**	o^{ow}t/nee^{oo}
old/young	**oud/jong**	o^{ow}t/yong
beautiful/ugly	**mooi/lelijk**	moa^{ee}/**lay**lerk
good/bad	**goed/slecht**	ghoot/slehkht
better/worse	**beter/slecht**	**bay**teer/slehkht

Some prepositions and a few more useful words

at	**te**	ter
on	**op**	op
in	**in**	in
to	**naar**	naar
from	**van**	vahn
inside	**binnen**	binnern
outside	**buiten**	bur^{ew}tern
up	**op**	op
down	**neer**	nayr
before	**voor**	voar
after	**na**	naa
with	**met**	meht
without	**zonder**	zonderr
through	**door**	doar
towards	**naar**	naar
until	**tot**	tot
during	**tijdens**	taiydernss
and	**en**	ehn
or	**of**	off
not	**niet**	neet
nothing	**niets**	neets
none	**geen**	ghayn
very	**zeer**	zayr
also	**ook**	oak
soon	**spoedig**	spooderkh
perhaps	**misschien**	mersskheen
here	**hier**	heer
there	**daar**	daar
now	**nu**	new
then	**dan**	dahn

Arrival

Passport control

Here is my passport.	**Hier is mijn paspoort.**	heer iss maiyn **pahs**poart
I'll be staying...	**Ik blijf hier...**	ik blaiyf heer
a few days	**een paar dagen**	ayn paar **daa**ghern
a week	**een week**	ayn ꝟayk
several weeks	**enkele weken**	**ehn**kerler **ꝟay**kern
I don't know yet.	**Ik weet het nog niet.**	ik ꝟayt heht nokh neet
I'm here on holiday.	**Ik ben hier met vakantie.**	ik behn heer meht vaa**kahn**see
I'm just passing through.	**Ik ben op doorreis.**	ik behn op **doar**raiyss
I'm sorry, I don't understand.	**Neemt u mij niet kwalijk, ik begrijp u niet.**	naymt ew maiy neet **kꝟaa**lerk ik ber**ghraiyp** ew neet
Is there anyone here who speaks English?	**Is er iemand hier die Engels spreekt?**	iss ehr **ee**mahnt heer dee **ehng**erlss spraykt

Customs

As at almost all major airports in Europe, an honour system for clearing customs has been adopted at Amsterdam's Schiphol airport. Baggage is often not even opened, although spot checks are a possibility. After collecting your baggage, you've a choice: follow the green arrow if you have nothing to declare. Or leave via a doorway marked with a red arrow if you have items to declare (in excess of those allowed).

niets aan te geven
nothing to declare

aangifte goederen
goods to declare

CAR/BORDER FORMALITIES, see page 146

The chart below shows what you can take in duty-free.*

	Cigarettes		Cigars		Tobacco	Spirits		Wine
European residents: bought outside EEC or inside EEC tax-free	200	or	50	or	250 g.	1 l.	and	2 l.
bought inside EEC countries not tax-free (Eur. residents)	300	or	75	or	400 g.	1½ l.	and	5 l.
for visitors from outside Europe	400	or	100	or	500 g.	1 l.	and	2 l.

Dutch customs may inquire about tea or coffee, since only a limited quantity of either is admitted duty-free.

I've nothing to declare.	**Ik heb niets aan te geven.**	ik hehp neets aan ter **ghay**vern
I've a...	**Ik heb een...**	ik hehp ayn
bottle of whisky/wine	**fles whisky/wijn**	flehss **ʋis**kee/ʋaiyn
carton of cigarettes	**slof sigaretten**	sloff seeghaa**reh**tern
It's for my personal use.	**Dit is voor mijn persoonlijk gebruik.**	dit iss voar maiyn pehr**soan**lerk gher**brur^{ew}k**
It's a present.	**Het is een cadeau.**	heht iss ayn kaa**doa**

Uw paspoort, alstublieft.	Your passport, please.
Hebt u iets aan te geven?	Have you anything to declare?
Wilt u deze tas even open maken?	Please open this bag.
U moet hiervoor invoerrechten betalen.	You'll have to pay duty on this.
Hebt u nog meer bagage?	Do you have any more luggage?

* All allowances are subject to change without notice.

Baggage—Porters

These days porters are only available at airports or the railway stations of large cities such as Amsterdam, Rotterdam, Utrecht and Antwerp. Where no porters are available, you'll find luggage trolleys for the use of passengers.

Porter!	**Kruier!**	krurᵉʷyerr
Please take these bags.	**Wilt u deze koffers meenemen, alstublieft.**	ʋilt ew **day**zer **koff**errss may**nay**mern ahlstew**bleeft**
That's mine.	**Die is van mij.**	dee iss vahn maiy
That's my suitcase.	**Dat is mijn koffer.**	daht iss maiyn **koff**err
That ... one.	**Die...**	dee
big/small	**grote/kleine**	**ghroa**ter/**klai**yner
black/check	**zwarte/geruite**	zʋ**ahr**ter/gher**rur**ᵉʷter
blue/brown	**blauwe/bruine**	**blo**ᵒʷʋer/**brur**ᵉʷner
There's one ... missing.	**Er ontbreekt een...**	ehr ont**braykt** ayn
bag	**reistas**	**raiyss**tahss
suitcase	**koffer**	**koff**err
Take these bags to...	**Breng deze reistassen naar...**	brehng **day**zer **raiyss**tahssern naar
the bus	**de bus**	der burss
the luggage lockers	**de bagagekluizen**	der baa**ghaa**zherklurᵉʷzern
the taxi	**de taxi**	der **tahk**see
How much is that?	**Hoeveel is het?**	hoo**vayl** iss heht
Where can I find a luggage trolley?	**Waar kan ik een bagagewagentje vinden?**	ʋaar kahn ik ayn baa**ghaa**zherʋaagherntyer **vin**dern

Changing money

At all airports and railway stations, you'll find a bank or *wisselkantoor* (currency-exchange office). Most of them stay open in the evening. In case you have trouble changing money late at night, your hotel might be able to help you.

See pages 134–136 for details of money and currency exchange and banking hours.

ARRIVAL

Where's the nearest currency exchange?	**Waar is het dichtstbijzijnde wisselkantoor?**	√aar iss heht dikhtst-baiy**zaiyn**der **√isserl**-kahntoar
Can you change these traveller's cheques (checks)?	**Kunt u deze reischeques inwisselen?**	kurnt ew **day**zer **raiys**-shehks in**√**isserlern
I want to change some ...	**Ik wil enige ... inwisselen.**	iik √il **ay**nergher ... in**√**isserlern
dollars	**dollars**	**dol**lahrss
pounds	**ponden**	**pon**dern
Can you change this into...?	**Kunt u dit tegen ... inwisselen?**	kurnt ew dit **taygh**ern... in**√**isserlern
guilders	**guldens**	**ghurl**dernss
Belgian francs	**Belgische franken**	**behl**gheesser **frahn**kern
What's the exchange rate?	**Wat is de wisselkoers?**	√aht iss der **√**isserlkoorss

Where?

All airports and most railway stations have information offices, and some even have a hotel reservation bureau.

Could you book a hotel room/room in a boarding house, please?	**Kunt u een hotelkamer/kamer in een pension voor mij reserveren?**	kurnt ew ayn hoa**tehl**-kaamerr/**kaa**merr in ayn pehn**syon** voar maiy rayzehr**vay**rern
in the centre	**in het centrum**	in heht **sehn**trurm
near the station	**bij het station**	baiy heht staht**syon**
for one person/ two people	**voor één person/ twee personen**	voar ayn pehr**soan**/ t√ay pehr**soa**nern
not too expensive	**niet te duur**	neet ter dewr
Where is the hotel/ boarding house?	**Waar is het hotel/ het pension?**	√aar iss heht hoa**tehl**/ heht pehn**syon**
Do you have a city map?	**Hebt u een stadsplan?**	hehpt ew ayn **stahts**plahn
How do I get to...?	**Hoe kom ik naar...?**	hoo kom ik naar

FOR NUMBERS, see page 175

Is there a bus into town?	**Gaat er een bus naar de stad?**	ghaat ehr ayn burss naar der staht
Where can I get a taxi?	**Waar kan ik een taxi vinden?**	ʋaar kahn ik ayn **tahksee vindern**
Where can I hire a car?	**Waar kan ik een auto huren?**	ʋaar kahn ik ayn o^{ow}toa **hew**rern

Car hire

There are car hire firms at most airports and terminals. There will most likely be someone who speaks English. But if this is not the case, try the following:

I'd like a...	**Ik wil graag een... huren.**	ik ʋil ghraakh ayn ... **hew**rern
car	**auto**	**o^{ow}**toa
small/large car	**kleine/grote auto**	**klaiy**ner/**ghroa**ter **o^{ow}**toa
I'd like it for...	**Ik wil het graag voor...**	ik ʋil heht ghraakh voar
a day/4 days	**één dag/4 dagen**	ayn dahkh/veer **daa**ghern
a week/2 weeks	**één week/2 weken**	ayn ʋayk/tʋay **ʋay**kern
What's the charge per day/week?	**Wat is het tarief per dag/week?**	ʋaht iss heht taa**reef** pehr dahkh/ʋayk
Does that include mileage?	**Is het aantal kilometers hierbij inbegrepen?**	iss heht **aan**tahl **kee**loamayterrs **heer**baiy **in**berghraypern
What's the charge per kilometre?	**Wat is het tarief per kilometer?**	ʋaht iss heht taa**reef** pehr **kee**loamayterr
Is petrol (gasoline) included?	**Is dat inclusief benzine?**	iss daht inklew**seef** behn**zee**ner
I want full insurance.	**Ik wil een all-risk verzekering, alstublieft.**	ik ʋil ayn "all-risk" vehr**zay**kerring ahlstew**bleeft**
What's the deposit?	**Hoeveel bedraagt de waarborgsom?**	hoovayl ber**draakht** der **ʋaar**borkhsom
I've a credit card.	**Ik heb een betaalpas.**	ik hehp ayn ber**taal**pahss
Here's my driving licence.	**Hier is mijn rijbewijs.**	heer iss maiyn **raiy**berʋaiyss

FOR SIGHTSEEING, see page 75

Taxi

In Holland, hailing a cab in the street is not a very common practice. You'll find taxi ranks at airports, railway stations and at various points in the cities. Meters are usually fitted to the dashboard of the taxi, showing the fare inclusive of tip. There is no extra charge for luggage or night trips. Rates may differ from place to place, it's usually best to ask the approximate fare beforehand.

Where can I get a taxi?	**Waar kan ik een taxi vinden?**	ʋaar kahn ik ayn **tahk**see vindern
Please get me a taxi.	**Wilt u een taxi voor mij bestellen?**	ʋilt ew ayn **tahk**see voar maiy ber**steh**lern
What's the fare to...?	**Wat kost het naar...?**	ʋaht kost heht naar
How far is it to...?	**Hoever is het naar...?**	hoo**vehr** iss heht naar
Take me to...	**Brengt u mij naar...**	brehngt ew maiy naar
this address	**dit adres**	dit aa**drehss**
the airport	**het vliegveld**	heht **vleegh**vehlt
the ... Hotel	**het ... Hotel**	heht ... hoa**tehl**
the station	**het station**	heht staht**syon**
the town centre	**het stadscentrum**	heht **staht**sehntrurm
Turn left/right at the next corner.	**Bij de volgende hoek linksaf/rechtsaf.**	baiy der **vol**ghernder hook **links**ahf/**rehkhts**ahf
Go straight ahead.	**Rechtuit, alstublieft.**	**rehkhtur^{ew}t** ahlstew**bleeft**
To the right/left at the traffic lights.	**Bij de stoplichten rechtsaf/linksaf.**	baiy der **stop**lightern **rehkhts**ahf/**links**ahf
Please stop here.	**Wilt u hier stoppen, alstublieft.**	ʋilt ew heer **stop**pern ahlstew**bleeft**
I'm in a hurry.	**Ik heb haast.**	ik hehp haast
I'm not in a hurry.	**Ik heb geen haast.**	ik hehp ghayn haast
Could you drive more slowly?	**Kunt u wat langzamer rijden, alstublieft?**	kurnt ew ʋaht **lahng**zaamerr **raiy**dern ahlstew**bleeft**
Would you help me carry my bags?	**Wilt u mij met mijn koffers helpen, alstublieft?**	ʋilt ew maiy meht maiyn **kof**ferrss **hehl**pern ahlstew**bleeft**

FOR TIPPING, see page 1

Hotel—Other accommodation

Particularly during the summer tourist season (April–September) it is highly advisable to reserve rooms well in advance. You may be asked to pay a deposit which could be claimed as compensation if the reservation is cancelled. Bookings can be made direct with the hotel of your choice, via a travel agency or airline, or through the National Reservation Centre (NCR). Most towns and arrival points have a tourist information office (VVV—*Vereniging voor Vreemdelingen Verkeer*), and that's the place to go if you're stuck without a room.

Hotel (hoa**tehl**) — Hotels in Holland are classified, first, according to category, from 1 (highest) to 5 (lowest), and secondly by a number of red stars. The categories concern the number of rooms, amenities, etc. (e.g. lifts, baths), whereas the red stars reflect the quality and comfort of a hotel (e.g. the location and the services offered). Thus a hotel shown as C1 (Class 1) with five stars would be a big hotel with maximum comfort and service in a beautiful location, while a hotel shown as C5 with no red stars would mean a small hotel with accommodation of the simplest type and virtually no service. Both category and number of stars may appear on a sign outside the hotel. Prices do not necessarily relate to this two-faceted classification.

Motel (moa**tehl**) — Motels are increasingly found near superhighways and other major roads.

Pension (pehn**syon**) — Many boarding houses are of a family nature. They normally offer *vol pension* (full board) or *half pension* (bed and breakfast plus one other meal). The local VVV office will supply you with addresses.

Zomerhuisje (**zoa**merrhur[ew]sher) — Bungalows can be rented in many tourist resorts, but you must book far in advance.

HOTEL

Jeugdherberg (**yurkh**thehrbehrkh) Youth hostels are open all year round to young people who are members of a youth hostel organization in their own country or hold an international youth hostel card.

In this section, we're mainly concerned with the smaller and medium-priced hotels and boarding houses. You'll have no language difficulties in the luxury and first-class hotels, where most of the staff speak English.

In the next few pages we consider your requirements—step by step—from arrival to departure.

Checking in—Reception

My name is …	**Mijn naam is …**	maiyn naam iss
I've a reservation.	**Ik heb gereserveerd.**	ik hehp gher**ray**zerrvayrt
We've reserved two rooms, a single and a double.	**Wij hebben twee kamers gereserveerd; een éénpersoonskamer en een tweepersoonskamer.**	ʋaiy **heh**bern tʋay **kaa**merrss gher**ray**zehrvayrt ayn **ayn**pehrsoanskaamerr ehn ayn **tʋay**pehrsoans-kaamerr
I wrote to you last month.	**Ik heb u vorige maand geschreven.**	ik hehp ew **voa**rergher maant gher**skhray**vern
Here's the confirmation.	**Hier is de bevestiging.**	heer iss der ber**veh**ster-ghing
I'd like a … room.	**Ik zou graag een … kamer willen hebben.**	ik zo^{ow} ghraakh ayn …**kaa**merr **ʋi**llern **heh**bern
single	**éénpersoons**	**ayn**pehrsoanss
double	**tweepersoons**	**tʋay**pehrsoanss
with twin beds	**met lits-jumeaux**	meht lee-zhew**mo^{ow}**
with a bath	**met badkamer**	meht **baht**kaamerr
with a shower	**met douche**	meht doosh
with a balcony	**met balkon**	meht bahl**kon**
with a view	**met uitzicht**	meht **ur^{ew}**tzikht
We'd like a room …	**Wij willen graag een kamer …**	ʋaiy **ʋi**llern ghraakh ayn **kaa**merr
in the front	**aan de voorkant**	aan der **voar**kahnt
at the back	**aan de achterkant**	aan der **ahkh**terrkahnt
facing the sea	**met uitzicht op de zee**	meht **ur^{ew}**tzikht op der zay

It must be quiet.	**Het moet er rustig zijn.**	heht moot ehr **rur**sterkh zaiyn
Is there ...?	**Is er ...?**	iss ehr
air conditioning	**air-conditioning**	**ehr**kondisherning
heating	**verwarming**	verr**ʋahr**ming
hot water	**warm water**	ʋahrm **ʋaa**terr
a laundry service	**een wasserij**	ayn ʋahsser**raiy**
a radio	**een radio**	ayn **raa**deeyoa
running water	**stromend water**	**stroa**mernt **ʋaa**terr
a television in the room	**een televisie op de kamer**	ayn tayler**vee**zee op der **kaa**merr
a private toilet	**een eigen toilet**	ayn **aiy**ghern tʋaa**leht**

How much?

What's the price ...?	**Hoeveel kost het ...?**	hoo**vayl** kost heht
per night	**per nacht**	pehr nakhkt
per week	**per week**	pehr ʋayk
for bed and breakfast	**voor overnachting met ontbijt**	voar oaverr**nahkh**ting meht ont**baiyt**
excluding meals	**zonder maaltijden**	zonderr **maal**taiydern
for full board	**voor vol pension**	voar vol pehn**syon**
for half board	**voor half pension**	voar hahlf pehn**syon**
Does that include ...?	**Is dat inclusief ...?**	iss daht inklew**seef**
breakfast	**ontbijt**	ont**baiyt**
service	**bediening**	ber**dee**ning
value-added tax (VAT)*	**B. T. W.**	bay-tay-ʋay
Is there any reduction for children?	**Is er een reductie voor kinderen?**	iss ehr ayn rer**durk**see voar **kin**derrern
Do you charge for the baby?	**Berekent u iets voor de baby?**	berr**ay**kernt ew eets voar der **bay**bee
That's too expensive.	**Dat is te duur.**	daht iss ter dewr
Haven't you anything cheaper?	**Hebt u niets goedkopers?**	hehpt ew neets ghoot**koa**perrss

* Americans note: a type of sales tax, called *B.T.W.* in Holland and Belgium. It's nearly always included in purchases, rentals, meals, etc.

FOR NUMBERS, see page 175

How long?

We'll be staying ...	**Wij blijven ...**	√aiy **blaiy**vern
overnight only	**alleen vannacht**	ah**layn** vahn**nahkht**
a few days	**een paar dagen**	ayn paar **daa**ghern
a week (at least)	**(minstens) een week**	(**min**sternss) ayn √ayk
I don't know yet.	**Ik weet het nog niet.**	ik √ayt heht nokh neet

Decision

May I see the room?	**Mag ik de kamer zien?**	mahkh ik der **kaa**merr zeen
No. I don't like it.	**Nee, die bevalt me niet.**	nay dee ber**vahlt** mer neet
It's too ...	**Hij is te ...**	heht iss ter
dark/small	**donker/klein**	**don**kerr/klaiyn
noisy	**lawaaierig**	laa**waa**^{ee}yerrerkh
I asked for a room with a bath.	**Ik heb om een kamer met bad gevraagd.**	ik hehp om ayn **kaa**merr meht baht gher**vraakht**
Do you have anything ...?	**Hebt u iets ...?**	hehpt ew eets
better	**beters**	**bay**terrss
bigger	**groters**	**ghroa**terrss
cheaper	**goedkopers**	ghoot**koa**perrss
quieter	**rustigers**	**rur**sterkherrss
Do you have a room with a better view?	**Hebt u een kamer met een beter uitzicht?**	hehpt ew ayn **kaa**merr meht ayn **bay**terr **ur**^{ew}**t**-zikht
That's fine. I'll take it.	**Deze is prima. Die neem ik.**	**day**zer iss **pree**mah. dee naym ik

The bill (check)

Usually, bills have to be paid weekly and of course upon departure if you stay less than a week. Some hotels might give a reduction for children under six. Find out about it when you make reservations.

FOR DAYS OF THE WEEK, see page 181

Service charges and tax (VAT) are normally included in the bill, but you can ask:

Is service included?	**Is het inclusief bediening?**	iss heht inklew**seef** ber**dee**ning

Tip the porter when he brings the bags to your room; tip the bellboy if he does any errands for you. So you should keep some small change at hand. (See also inside back-cover.)

Registration

Upon arrival at a hotel or boarding house you'll be asked to fill in a registration form (*aanmeldingsformulier*—**aan**mehldingsformewleer). It asks your name, home address, passport number and further destination. It's almost certain to carry an English translation. If it doesn't, ask the desk-clerk (*de receptionist*—rerssehpseeyo**nist**):

What does this mean?	**Wat betekent dit?**	vaht ber**tay**kernt dit

The desk-clerk will also ask you for your passport. If you don't understand what he is saying, show him the section below:

Mag ik uw paspoort even zien?	May I see your passport, please?
Zoudt u zo vriendelijk willen zijn dit formulier in te vullen?	Would you mind filling in this registration form?
Hier tekenen, alstublieft.	Please sign here.
Hoelang bent u van plan te blijven?	How long will you be staying?

What's my room number?	**Wat is mijn kamernummer?**	vaht iss maiyn **kaa**merrnurmerr
Will you have my/our bags sent up?	**Wilt u mijn/onze bagage naar boven laten brengen?**	vilt ew maiyn/**on**zer baa**ghaa**zher naar **boa**vern **laa**tern **brehn**gern

Service, please

Now that you are safely installed, meet the other members of the hotel staff:

bellboy	**de piccolo**	der **pee**koaloa
maid	**het kamermeisje**	heht **kaa**merrmaiysher
manager	**de direkteur**	der deerehk**turr**
switchboard operator	**de telefoniste**	der taylerfoa**nis**ter
waiter	**de kelner**	der **kehl**nerr
waitress	**de serveerster**	der sehr**vayr**sterr

Call the members of the staff *Juffrouw* (**yur**fro^{ow})—Miss, or *Mevrouw* (mer**vro^{ow}**)—Madam, and *Mijnheer* (mer**nayr**)—Sir. Address the waiter as *Ober* (**oa**berr) when calling for service.

General requirements

Please ask the maid to come up.	**Wilt u het kamermeisje vragen boven te komen?**	ʋilt ew heht **kaa**merr-maiysher **vraa**ghern **boa**vern ter **koa**mern
Just a minute.	**Een ogenblikje.**	ayn **oa**ghernblikyer
Come in!	**Binnen!**	binnern
Is there a bath on this floor?	**Is er een badkamer op deze verdieping?**	iss ehr ayn **baht**kaamerr op **day**zer verr**dee**ping
Could you send up ..., please?	**Kunt u ... boven laten brengen, alstublieft?**	kurnt ew ... **boa**vern **laa**tern **breh**ngern ahlstew**bleeft**
two cups of coffee	**twee kopjes koffie**	tʋay **kop**yerss **ko**ffee
a sandwich	**een sandwich**	ayn "sandwich"
Can we have breakfast in our room?	**Kunnen we in onze kamer ontbijten?**	**kur**nnern ʋer in **on**zer **kaa**merr ont**bai**ytern
I'd like to leave these in your safe.	**Ik wil dit graag in de hotel-kluis deponeren.**	ik ʋil dit ghraakh in der hoa**tehl**-klur^{ew}ss daypoa**nay**rern
Can you get me a babysitter?	**Kunt u een babysitter voor mij krijgen?**	kurnt ew ayn "babysitter" voar maiy **krai**yghern

May I have a/an ...?	**Kan ik ... krijgen?**	kahn ik ... **kraiyghern**
ashtray	**een asbak**	ayn **ahs**bahk
bath towel	**een badhanddoek**	ayn **baht**hahndook
extra blanket	**een extra deken**	ayn **ehk**straa **day**kern
envelopes	**enveloppen**	ehnverloppern
(more) hangers	**(nog) een paar kleerhangers**	(nokh) ayn paar **klayr**hahngerrss
hot-water bottle	**een kruik**	ayn krur^{ew}k
ice cubes	**ijsblokjes**	**aiys**blokyerss
needle and thread	**naald en draad**	naalt ehn draat
reading-lamp	**een bedlampje**	ayn **beht**lampyer
soap	**zeep**	zayp
writing-paper	**schrijfpapier**	**skhraiyf**paapeer
Where's the ...?	**Waar is ...?**	Ѵaar iss
bathroom	**de badkamer**	der **baht**kaamerr
cocktail lounge	**de bar**	der bahr
dining-room	**de eetzaal**	der **ayt**zaal
hairdresser's	**de kapper**	der **kah**perr
restaurant	**het restaurant**	heht rehstoa**rahnt**
telephone	**de telefoon**	der tayler**foan**
television room	**de televisiekamer**	der taylerv**eezee**kaamerr
toilet	**het toilet**	heht t**Ѵaaleht**

Breakfast

The Dutch breakfast, or *ontbijt*, consists of coffee or tea, three or four types of bread or rolls (*broodjes*—**broa**tyerss), thin slices of cheese or ham, preserves and sometimes a boiled egg. Most of the larger hotels, however, are now used to providing an English or American breakfast.

I'll have some ...	**Ik wil graag ... hebben.**	ik Ѵil ghraakh ... **heh**bern
cocoa	**cacao**	**kaako^{ow}**
coffee	**koffie**	**ko**ffee
black	**zwarte**	z**Ѵahr**ter
with cream	**met room**	meht roam
with milk	**met melk**	meht mehlk
decaffeinated	**cafeïnevrije**	kahfay**ee**nervraiyyer
juice	**sap**	sahp
grapefruit	**grapefruit**	"grapefruit"
orange	**sinaasappel**	**see**naasahperl
tomato	**tomaten**	toa**maa**tern

FOR EATING OUT, see pages 38–64

milk	**melk**	mehlk
hot/cold	**warme/koude**	**√ahr**mer/**ko^{ow}**der
skimmed	**taptemelk**	**tahp**termehlk
tea	**thee**	tay
with milk	**met melk**	meht mehlk
with lemon	**met citroen**	meht see**troon**
May I have a/an some ...?	**Mag ik ... hebben?**	mahkh ik ... **heh**bern
bacon and eggs	**spiegeleieren met ontbijtspek**	**spee**gherlaiyerrern meht ont**baiyt**spehk
boiled egg	**een gekookt ei**	ayn gher**koakt** aiy
hard	**hard**	hahrt
medium	**medium**	**mee**deeyurm
soft	**zacht**	zahkht
bread	**wat broot**	√aht broat
butter	**wat boter**	√aht **boa**terr
cereals	**wat cornflakes**	√aht **korn**flayks
cheese	**wat kaas**	√aht kaass
crispbread	**wat beschuit**	√aht ber**skhur^{ew}t**
honey	**wat honing**	√aht **hoa**ning
marmalade	**wat marmelade**	√aht mahrmaer**laa**der
rolls	**een paar broodjes**	ayn paar **broa**tyerss
toast	**wat toast**	√aht toast
yoghurt	**wat joghurt**	√aht **yok**hurrt
Could you bring me a/some ...?	**Kunt u mij ... brengen?**	kurnt ew maiy ... **breh**ngen
cream	**wat room**	√aht roam
lemon	**wat citroen**	√aht see**troon**
pepper	**wat peper**	√aht **pay**perr
saccharin	**wat saccharine**	√aht sahkhaa**ree**ner
salt	**wat zout**	√aht zo^{ow}t
sugar	**wat suiker**	√aht **sur^{ew}**ker
glass of water	**een glas water**	ayn glahss **√aa**terr
hot water	**wat warm water**	√aht √ahrm **√aa**terr

Difficulties

The ... doesn't work.	**... werkt niet.**	... √ehrkt neet
fan	**de ventilator**	der vehntee**laa**tor
heating	**de verwarming**	der verr**√ahr**ming
light	**het licht**	heht likht
radiator	**de radiateur**	der raadeeyaa**turr**
radio	**de radio**	der **raa**deeyoa

shower	**de douche**	der doosh
tap	**de kraan**	der kraan
television set	**de televisie**	der tayler**veezee**
toilet	**het toilet**	heht t**ʋaaleht**
ventilator	**de ventilatie**	der vehntee**laatsee**
The wash-basin is clogged.	**De wastafel is verstopt.**	der **ʋahs**taaferl iss verr**stopt**
The window is jammed.	**Het raam klemt.**	heht raam klehmt
The blind is stuck.	**De jaloezie zit vast.**	der yaaloo**zee** zit vahst
These aren't my shoes.	**Dit zijn mijn schoenen niet.**	dit zaiyn maiyn **skhoo**nern neet
This isn't my laundry.	**Dit is mijn wasgoed niet.**	dit iss maiyn **ʋahs**ghoot neet
There's no hot water.	**Er is geen warm water.**	ehr iss ghayn ʋahrm **ʋaa**terr
I've lost my watch.	**Ik heb mijn horloge verloren.**	ik hehp maiyn hor**loa**zher verr**loa**rern
I've left my key in my room.	**Ik heb mijn sleutel in mijn kamer laten liggen.**	ik hehp maiyn **slur**terl in maiyn **kaa**merr **laa**tern **ligh**ern
The bulb is burnt out.	**De lamp is gesprongen.**	der lamp iss gher**sprong**ern
The ... is broken.	**... is kapot.**	... iss kaa**pot**
lamp	**het licht**	heht likht
plug	**het stopkontakt**	heht **stop**kontahkt
shutter	**het luik**	heht lur^{ew}k
switch	**de schakelaar**	der **skhaa**kerlaar
venetian blind	**de store**	der stoar
window shade	**het zonnescherm**	heht **zon**nerskhehrm
Can you get it repaired?	**Kunt u het laten repareren?**	kurnt ew heht **laa**tern raypaa**ray**rern

Telephone—Mail

Can you get me Amsterdam 311-34-67?	**Kunt u me met Amsterdam 311-34-67 verbinden?**	kurnt ew mer meht ahmsterr**dahm** 311-34-67 verr**bin**dern
Are there any messages for me?	**Zijn er boodschappen voor mij?**	zaiyn ehr **boat**shahpern voar maiy

FOR POST OFFICE AND TELEPHONE, see pages 137–141

Have you received any mail for me?	**Hebt u post voor mij ontvangen?**	hehpt ew post voar maiy ont**vahn**gern
Do you have stamps?	**Hebt u postzegels?**	hehpt ew post**zay**gherlss
Would you please mail this for me?	**Wilt u dit voor mij posten, alstublieft?**	vilt ew dit voar maiy **pos**tern ahlstew**bleeft**

Checking out

May I please have my bill?	**Mag ik mijn rekening, alstublieft?**	mahkh ik maiyn **ray**kerning ahlstew**bleeft**
I'm leaving early tomorrow. Please have my bill ready.	**Ik vertrek morgenochtend vroeg. Wilt u mijn rekening klaarmaken, alstublieft?**	ik verr**trehk** morghern**okh**ternt vrookh. vilt ew maiyn **ray**kerning **klaar**maakern ahlstew**bleeft**
We'll be checking out around noon/soon.	**Wij vertrekken omstreeks 12 uur/spoedig.**	vaiy verr**treh**kern **om**strayks tvaalf ewr/**spoo**derkh
I must leave at once.	**Ik moet onmiddellijk vertrekken.**	ik moet on**mid**derlerk verr**treh**kern
Is everything included?	**Is alles inbegrepen?**	iss **ah**lerss **in**berghraypern
You've made a mistake in this bill, I think.	**Ik geloof, dat u een vergissing in de rekening gemaakt hebt.**	ik gher**loaf** daht ew ayn verr**ghis**sing in der **ray**kerning gher**maakt** hehpt
Can you get us a taxi?	**Kunt u een taxi voor ons bestellen?**	kurnt ew ayn **tah**ksee voar onss ber**steh**lern
When's the next ... to Brussels?	**Wanneer vertrekt de/het volgende ... naar Brussel?**	vah**nayr** verr**trehkt** der/het **vol**ghender ... naar **brur**sserl
bus/plain/train	**bus/vliegtuig/trein**	burss/**vleegh**tur^{ew}kh/traiyn
Would you send someone to bring down our baggage?	**Wilt u onze bagage naar beneden laten brengen?**	vilt ew **on**zer baa**ghaa**zher naar ber**nay**dern **laa**tern **breh**ngern
We're in a great hurry.	**Wij hebben erge haast.**	vaiy **heh**bern **ehr**gher haast
Here's my forwarding address. You have my home address.	**Hier is mijn volgende adres. Mijn huisadres hebt u al.**	heer iss maiyn **vol**ghernder aa**drehss.** maiyn **hur^{ew}ss**aadrehss hehpt ew ahl

FOR TIPPING, see page 1

Eating out

There are many different types of eating and drinking places in Holland and the restaurants, especially in Amsterdam, are as varied in atmosphere as in menu.

Bar (bahr)	A sophisticated drinking place, where all sorts of drinks are served.
Bistro (beestroa)	A cosy place to eat, where special, tasty meals are served.
Broodjeswinkel (broatyers√inkerl)	A sandwich shop; serves a great variety of sandwiches made of *broodjes* (rolls) with different types of meat, fish and cheese. This is one of the Dutchman's favourite places for lunch or a quick snack.
Café (kahfay)	This is the place where the Dutch go to have a drink and to play billiards.
Cafetaria (kahfertayreeyaa)	Serves hot meals and is often self-service.
Hotel (hoatehl)	Most hotel restaurants are open to the public.
Koffieshop (koffeeshop)	A coffee-house where the Dutch go for their *kopje koffie* (cup of coffee) and *gebak* (pastries) in the morning.
Motel or Weg-restaurant (moatehl √eghrehstoarahnt)	Eating places along the major highways; international choice of food.
Nachtclub (nahkhtklurp)	A nightclub, generally with a floor show and strip-tease.
Pannekoekhuisje (pahnerkookhurewsher)	A pancake-house serving a wide variety of *flensjes* (a thin type of pancake) and *pannekoeken* (pancakes). You could also try *poffertjes* (a kind of small round pancake) which are served with butter and powder sugar.
Proeflokaal (proofloakaal)	A bar/shop where you can sample (but not free) various local drinks. Here you can try *jenever* (Dutch gin). There are also lemon-, redcurrant- and blackberry-flavoured jenevers. Just ask for a *borreltje* (glass of jenever).

Restaurant (rehstoa**rahnt**)
Many restaurants in Holland specialize in French, Italian, Indonesian, Greek, Japanese, Indian and Turkish cooking. A few of them even advertise *Dutch restaurant,* in English, on the door.

Snackbar
Useful for a bite on the run. For snacks, see page 62.

Tea-room
These serve tea and coffee. The Dutch like to take their tea between 3 and 5 p.m. with *koekjes* (biscuits) or *gebak* (pastry).

Meal times

Breakfast (*ontbijt*—ont**baiyt**) is generally served between 7 and 10 a.m. See page 34 for a breakfast menu.

Lunch is generally served from noon until 2 p.m. The *koffietafel* (**ko**ffeetaaferl) is a sandwich lunch (including coffee, milk or tea), consisting of various types of bread, cold meats, cheese and possibly a warm dish, and preceded by a bowl of soup or a salad.

Dinner (*diner*—dee**nay**) is usually served between 6 and 8 p.m.

BTW en bediening inbegrepen. These words simplify your life as a tourist in Holland. They mean: Value Added Tax and service charge included. But it's customary to round off payment or give an extra guilder or two if service has been particularly good.

Eating habits

Most restaurants display a menu in the window. Look for the *dagschotel*—**dahkh**skhoaterl (daily special), which is usually a simple but tasty dish at a reasonable price. Some 750 restaurants throughout Holland offer a tourist menu, consisting of an appetizer, a main course and a dessert, for quite a modest sum. These restaurants can be recognized by the emblem shown here.

Hungry

I'm hungry/I'm thirsty.	**Ik heb honger/Ik heb dorst.**	ik hehp **hong**err/ik hehp dorst
Can you recommend a good restaurant?	**Kunt u een goed restaurant aanbevelen?**	kurnt ew ayn ghoot rehstoa**rahnt aan**bervaylern
Are there any inexpensive restaurants around here?	**Zijn er hier goedkope restaurants in de buurt?**	zaiyn ehr heer ghoot**koaper** rehstoa**rahnts** in der bewrt

To be sure of getting a table in a well-known restaurant, it's advisable to telephone in advance.

I'd like to reserve a table for 4. We'll come at 8.	**Ik wil graag een tafel voor 4 personen reserveren. Wij komen om 8 uur.**	ik ʋil ghraakh ayn **taa**ferl voar 4 pehr**soa**nern rayzehr**vay**rern. ʋaiy **koa**mern om 8 ewr

Wat wenst u?	What would you like?
Ik kan u dit aanbevelen.	I recommend this.
Wat wilt u drinken?	What would you like to drink?
Wij hebben geen ...	We haven't got ...
Wilt u ...?	Do you want ...

Asking and ordering

Good evening. I'd like a table for 2.	**Goedenavond. Ik wil graag een tafel voor 2 personen.**	ghoodern**aa**vont. ik ʋil ghraakh ayn **taa**ferl voar 2 pehr**soa**nern
Could we have a table ...?	**Kunnen wij een tafel ... krijgen?**	**kur**nnern ʋaiy ayn **taa**ferl ... **krai**ghern
in the corner	**in de hoek**	in der hook
by the window	**bij het raam**	baiy heht raam
outside	**buiten**	**bur^{ew}**tern
on the terrace	**op het terras**	op heht teh**rahss**

Are these places taken?	**Zijn deze plaatsen bezet?**	zaiyn dayzer **plaat**sern ber**zeht**
Waiter/Waitress!	**Ober/Juffrouw!**	oaberr/yurfro[ow]
We'd like something to eat/drink.	**We willen graag iets eten/drinken.**	ver **vil**lern ghraakh eets **ay**tern/**drin**kern
Could I have the menu/wine list?	**Mag ik de spijs-kaart/wijnkaart hebben?**	mahkh ik der **spaiyss**kaart/ **vaiyn**kaart **heh**bern
What's this?	**Wat is dit?**	vaht iss dit
Do you have ...?	**Hebt u ...?**	hehpt ew
a set menu	**een menu**	ayn mer**new**
local dishes	**speciale gerechten van deze streek**	spaysyaaler gher**rehkh**tern vahn **day**zer strayk
Is service included?	**Is het inclusief bediening?**	iss heht inklew**seef** ber**dee**ning
Could you serve me straight away, please? I'm in a hurry.	**Kunt u me meteen bedienen, alstu-blieft? Ik heb haast.**	kurnt ew mer mer**tayn** ber**dee**nern ahlstew**bleeft** ik hehp haast
Could I have an extra plate for the child?	**Mag ik een extra bord voor dit kind hebben?**	mahkh ik ayn **ehk**straa bort voar dit kint **heh**bern
Could we have a/an/ some ..., please?	**Kunnen we een ... krijgen?**	**kur**nern ver ayn ... **kraiy**ghern
ashtray	**asbak**	**ahs**bahk
another chair	**nog een stoel**	nokh ayn stool
bottle of ...	**fles ...**	flehss
fork	**vork**	vork
glass	**glas**	ghlahss
glass of water	**glas water**	ghlahss **vaa**terr
knife	**mes**	mehss
matches	**lucifers**	**lew**sseefehrss
napkin	**servet**	sehr**veht**
plate	**bord**	bort
serviette	**servet**	sehr**veht**
spoon	**lepel**	**lay**perl
toothpick	**tandestoker**	**tahn**derstoakerr
I'd like a/an/ some...	**Ik wil graag ... hebben.**	ik vil ghraakh ... **heh**bern
aperitif	**een aperitief**	ayn aapayree**teef**
appetizer	**een voorgerecht**	ayn **voar**gherrehkht

FOR COMPLAINTS, see page 58

beer	**een biertje**	ayn **beer**tyer
bread	**wat brood**	ʋaht broat
butter	**boter**	**boa**terr
cheese	**kaas**	kaass
chips	**patates frites**	paa**taht** freet
coffee	**een kopje koffie**	ayn **kop**yer **kof**fee
dessert	**een nagerecht**	ayn **naa**gherrehkht
fish	**vis**	viss
french fries	**patates frites**	paa**taht** freet
fruit	**fruit**	frur[ew]t
fruit-juice	**vruchtesap**	**vrurkh**ternsahp
game	**gevogelte**	gher**voa**gherlter
ice-cream	**ijs**	aiyss
ketchup	**wat ketchup**	ʋaht keht**shurp**
lemon	**citroen**	see**troon**
lettuce	**een kropsla**	ayn krop**slaa**
meat	**vlees**	vlayss
milk	**een glas melk**	ayn glahss mehlk
mineral water	**mineraalwater**	meener**raal**ʋaaterr
mustard	**mosterd**	**mos**terrt
oil	**wat olie**	ʋaht **oa**lee
olive oil	**wat olijfolie**	ʋaht oa**laiyf**oalee
pasta	**piment**	pee**mehnt**
pepper	**peper**	**pay**perr
potatoes	**aardappels**	**aar**dahperlss
poultry	**kip**	kip
rice	**rijst**	raiyst
rolls	**een paar broodjes**	ayn paar **broa**tyerss
salad	**sla**	slaa
salt	**zout**	zo[ow]t
saccharin	**saccharine**	sahkhaa**ree**ner
sandwich	**een sandwich**	ayn "sandwich"
seafood	**schaal- en schelp-dieren**	skhaal ehn **skhehlp**deeren
seasoning	**wat kruiden**	ʋaht **krur[ew]**dern
soft drink	**een frisdrank**	ayn **fris**drahnk
soup	**soep**	soop
spaghetti	**spaghetti**	spaa**kheh**tee
starter	**een voorgerecht**	ayn **voar**gherrekht
sugar	**suiker**	**sur[ew]**kerr
tea	**een kopje thee**	ayn **kop**yer tay
vegetables	**groenten**	**ghroon**tern
vinegar	**wat azijn**	ʋaht aa**zaiyn**
(iced) water	**(ijs)water**	(aiys) **ʋaa**terr
wine	**wijn**	ʋaiyn

EATING OUT

What's on the menu?

Our menu is presented according to courses. Under the headings below you'll find alphabetical lists of dishes likely to be offered on a Dutch menu, with their English equivalents. You can also show the book to the waiter. If you want some fruit, for instance, show him the appropriate list and let him point to what's available. Use pages 40–42 for ordering in general.

Typical Dutch cooking can "stick your ribs together": the Dutch like hearty meals, especially when the weather is cold. In most restaurants you'll find a choice of international dishes. Centuries of Dutch colonial presence in what is now Indonesia have added another dimension to the cuisine of the Netherlands. Rice-based, sometimes spicy Indonesian and Chinese-influenced food is found in many specialized restaurants throughout the country, in towns and sometimes even villages as well as in the large cities.

Here, then is our guide to good eating and drinking. Turn to the section you want.

Appetizers

I'd like an appetizer.	**Ik wil graag een voorgerecht hebben.**	ik √il ghraakh ayn **voar**gherrekht **heh**bern
What do you recommend?	**Wat beveelt u mij/ons aan?**	√aht ber**vaylt** ew maiy/onss aan
aspergepunten	ahs**pehr**zherpurntern	asparagus tips
bitterballen	**bit**terrbahlern	small round breaded meatballs
champignons op toast	shahmpee**ñonss** op toast	mushrooms on toast
croquetten (ham, kaas, kip, vlees, garnalen)	kroa**keh**tern (hahm kaass kip vlayss ghahr**naa**lern)	croquettes (ham, cheese, chicken, meat, shrimps)
eieren	**aiy**yerrern	eggs
gevulde	gher**vurl**der	stuffed
Russische	**rurs**seesser	Russian
garnalen	ghahr**naa**lern	shrimps
garnalencocktail	ghahr**naa**lernkoktayl	shrimp cocktail
gevarieerde hors d'œuvre	ghervaaree**yayr**der hor dervr	assorted appetizers
haring	**haa**ring	herring
nieuwe/gerookte	**nee**°°√er/gher**roak**ter	raw/smoked
kaasbroodje	**kaass**broatyer	Welsh rarebit
kaviaar	kaavee**yaar**	caviar
kievitseieren	**keeveets**aiyyerrern	plover's eggs
krabcoctail	**krahp**koktayl	crabmeat cocktail
kreeft	krayft	lobster
kreeftecocktail	**krayf**terkoktayl	lobster cocktail
makreel (gemarineerd)	maa**krayl** (ghermaaree**nayrt**)	mackerel (soused)
meloen	mer**loon**	melon
mosselen	**mos**serlern	mussels
oesters	**oos**terrss	oysters
paling	**paa**ling	eel
gerookte	gher**roak**ter	smoked
gesmoorde	gher**smoar**der	stewed
pastei	pahs**taiy**	pâté
pasteitje	pahs**taiy**tyer	pastry shell filled with sweetbreads, chicken or veal
schelvislever	**skhehl**vislayverr	haddock liver
soufflé	soof**flay**	soufflé
asperge	ahs**pehr**zher	asparagus
ham	hahm	ham
kaas	kaass	cheese

tomaten	toamaatern	tomatoes
gevulde	ghervurlder	stuffed
zalm	zahlm	salmon
gerookte	gherroakter	smoked

The Dutch make a lot of their snacks, or *borrelhapjes* (**bor**rerlhahpyerss), when inviting guests for drinks: small portions of toast surmounted with various garnishes; small pieces of vegetables with dips; *zebras*—layers of rye bread alternating with cream-cheese, cut in small sections, etc.

Salads

The Dutch sometimes take these salads as part of their *koffietafel* (see p. 39).

What salads do you have?	**Welke soorten salade hebt u?**	**veh**lker **soa**rtern saa**laa**der hehpt ew
aspergesalade	ahspehrzhersaalaader	asparagus, egg, pickles, ham, radishes
haringsalade	haaringsaalaader	herring, beetroot, apple, potato, pickles and mayonnaise
huzarensalade	hewzaarernsaalaader	potato, hard-boiled egg, mayonnaise and pickles
Italiaanse salade	eetaalyaanser saalaader	mixed salad with tomato, olives and tunny fish

Eggs and omelets

omelet	ommerleht	omelet
boerenomelet	boorernommerleht	with diced vegetables and bacon
fines herbes	feen zehrb	with herbs
met champignons	meht shahmpeeñonss	with mushrooms
met ham	meht hahm	with ham
met kaas	meht kaass	with cheese
met kippelevertjes	meht kipperlayverrtyerss	with chicken livers
roerei	rooraiy	scrambled eggs
spiegeleieren met ham	speegherlaiyyerrern meht hahm	ham and eggs

Soup

Soups are an important part of Dutch cooking. They are either served as a hot dish with the traditional Dutch *koffietafel* (see p. 39) or as the first course of the main meal. Two types of soup can be found on menus: *heldere soep* consommé or clear soup), and *gebonden soep* (cream). Sometimes the French word *potage* is used.

aardappelsoep	**aar**dahperlsoop	potato soup
aspergesoep	ahs**pehr**zhersoop	asparagus soup
bisque de homard	beesk der om**maar**	lobster chowder
bloemkoolsoep	**bloom**koalsoop	cauliflower soup
bouillon	boo^{ee}**yon**	broth
met croutons	meht kroo**tonss**	with fried bread cubes
met eiergelei	meht **aiy**yerrzherlaiy	with an egg (consommé royal)
met groenten	meht **ghroon**tern	with chopped vegetables (consommé julienne)
met omelet	meht ommer**leht**	with thin shreds of omelet (consommé célestine)
bruine bonensoep	**brur**^{ew}ner **boa**nernsoop	bean soup
champignonsoep	shahmpee**ñon**soop	mushroom soup
erwtensoep	**ehr**ternsoop	thick pea soup (see specialities)
Franse uiensoep	**frahn**ser **ur**^{ew}yernsoop	French onion soup
groentesoep (met balletjes)	**ghroon**ternsoop (meht **bah**llertyerss)	vegetable soup (with meat-balls)
kervelsoep	**kehr**verlsoop	chervil soup
kippesoep	**kip**persoop	chicken soup
koninginnesoep	koaniy**in**nersoop	cream of chicken
kreeftesoep	**kray**ftersoop	lobster chowder
Londonderrysoep	london**dehr**reesoop	Londonderry soup: creamy soup with hot spices
oestersoep	**oos**terrsoop	oyster soup
ossestaartsoep	**os**serstaartsoop	oxtail soup
palingsoep	**paa**lingsoop	cream of eel
preisoep	**praiy**soop	cream of leeks
soep van de dag	soop vahn der dahkh	soup of the day
spinaziesoep	speen**aa**zeesoop	spinach soup
schildpadsoep	**skhilt**pahtsoop	mock turtle
vermicellisoep	vehrmer**seh**leesoop	clear noodle soup

Fish and seafood

Even though it may sound a little too exotic for your taste at first hearing, salted raw herring—called "new herring" (*nieuwe haring* or *Hollandse nieuwe*)—is a treat not to be missed during the first weeks of May. The Dutch traditionally buy it at street stalls, but it is also served in restaurants. The big Zeeland oysters and mussels are mainly available from September to March.

I'd like some fish.	**Ik wil graag vis hebben.**	ik √il ghraakh viss **heh**bern
What kinds of fish do you have?	**Welke soorten vis hebt u?**	**√ehl**ker **soar**ten viss hehpt ew

baars	baarss	perch
bokking	**bok**king	kipper
bot	bot	flounder
brasem	**braa**zerm	bream
forel	foa**rehl**	trout
garnalen	ghahr**naa**lern	shrimp
griet	ghreet	brill
haring	**haa**ring	herring
heek	hayk	hake
heilbot	**haiyl**bot	halibut
kabeljouw	kahber**lyo^ow**	cod
karper	**kahr**pehr	carp
knorhaan	**knor**haan	gurnard
krab	krahp	crab
kreeft	krayft	lobster
maatjesharing	**maa**tyershaaring	matie, maty
makreel	maa**krayl**	mackerel
mosselen	**mos**serlern	mussels
oesters	**oos**terr	oysters
paling	**paa**ling	eel
pelser	**pehl**zerr	pilchard
poon (grote)	poan (**ghroa**ter)	sapphirine gurnard
poon (kleine)	poan (**klaiy**ner)	grey gurnard
rivierkreeft	ree**veer**krayft	crayfish
sardines	sahr**dee**nerss	sardines
schar	skhahr	dab
schelvis	**skhehl**viss	haddock
schol	skhol	plaice
snoek	snook	pike
snoekbaars	**snook**baarss	perch-pike
sprot	sprot	sprats

tarbot	tah**r**bot	turbot
tong	tong	sole
tongschar	**tong**skhahr	lemon sole
tonijn	toa**naiyn**	tuna
wijting	ѵ**aiy**ting	whiting
witvis	ѵ**it**viss	whitebait
zalm	zahlm	salmon
zeebaars	**zay**baarss	bass
zeeforel	**zay**foarehl	seatrout
zeehaan	**zay**haan	(red) mullet
zeekreeft (kleine)	**zay**krayft (**klai**yner)	scampi
zeelt	zaylt	tench
zeepaling	**zay**paaling	conger eel
zeewolf	**zay**ѵolf	catfish

baked	**in de oven gebakken**	in der **oa**vern gher**bah**kern
fried	**gebakken**	gher**bah**kern
grilled	**geroosterd/gegrilleerd**	gher**roa**sterrt/ gherghree**yayrt**
marinated	**gemarineerd**	ghermaaree**nayrt**
poached	**gekookt/gepocheerd**	gher**koakt**/gherpo**shayrt**
sautéed	**snel aangebraden**	snehl **aan**gherbraadern
smoked	**gerookt**	gher**roakt**
steamed	**gestoofd**	gher**stoaft**
stewed	**gesmoord**	gher**smoart**

Fish specialities

Gerookte paling (gher**roak**ter **paa**ling) delicately smoked eel, served on toast or with potatoes and salad

Haring, or **Hollandse nieuwe** (**haa**ring, **hol**lahntser **nee**ººѵer) filleted, salted herring. Hold it by the tail, dip it in chopped onions and gobble it down like a true Dutchman—or Dutchwoman!

Mosselen (**mos**serlern) mussels served with a mustard sauce and chips (french fries).

Rolmops (**rol**mops) rolled up fillets of herring marinated in spiced vinegar

Stokvis (**stok**viss) stockfish: dried cod with rice, fried potatoes and onions, mustard sauce

Zure haring (**zew**rer **haa**ring) marinated herring, served on bread or toast

EATING OUT

Meat

I'd like some…	**Ik wil graag … hebben.**	ik ʋil ghraakh … **heh**bern
beef/lamb	**rundvlees/lamsvlees**	**rurnt**vlayss/**lahms**vlayss
pork/veal	**varkensvlees/ kalfsvlees**	**vahr**kehnsvlayss/ **kahlfs**vlayss
biefstuk	**beef**sturk	fillet of beef
biefstuk tartare	**beef**sturk	steak tartare
blinde vinken	**blin**der **vin**kern	stuffed fillets of veal
borststuk	**borst**sturk	breast
braadworst	**braat**ʋorst	frying sausage
contre-filet	kontr-fee**leh**	sirloin steak
Duitse biefstuk	**dur^{ew}tser beef**sturk	hamburger steak
entrecôte	ahntrer**koat**	rib-steak
gehakt	gher**hahkt**	minced meat
gehaktbal	gher**hahkt**bahl	meat-ball
hachee	hah**shay**	stew served with potatoes
Hollandse biefstuk	**hol**lahntser **beef**sturk	loin cut of T-bone steak
kalfsborst	**kahlfs**borst	breast of veal
kalfshaas	**kahlfs**haass	tenderloin of veal
kalfskotelet	**kahlfs**koaterleht	veal cutlet
kalfsoester	**kahlfs**oosterrss	thin fillet of veal
karbonade	kahrboa**naa**der	chop
kotelet	koater**leht**	cutlet
lamsbout	**lahms**bo^{ow}t	leg of lamb
lamskarbonades	**lahms**kahrboanaader	lamb chops
lever	**lay**verr	liver
niertjes	**neer**tyerss	kidneys
ossestaart	**os**serstaart	oxtail
rolpens	**rol**pehnss	tripe
rookworst	**roak**ʋorst	smoked sausage
rosbief	**ros**beef	roast beef
saucijsjes	soa**saiy**sherss	sausages
schapevlees	**skhaa**pervlayss	mutton
schouderstuk	**skho^{ow}**derrsturk	shoulder
spek	spehk	bacon
tong	tong	tongue
tournedos	toorner**doa**	thick round fillet cut of prime beef
varkenshaas	**vahr**kernshaass	fillet of pork
varkenskarbonade	**vahr**kernskahrboanaader	pork chop
worst	ʋorst	sausage
zwezerik	**zʋay**zerrik	sweetbreads

How do you like your meat?

baked	**in de oven gebakken**	in der oavern gher**bah**kern
boiled	**gekookt**	gher**koakt**
braised	**gesmoord**	gher**smoart**
fried	**gebraden**	gher**braa**dern
grilled	**geroosterd**	gher**roa**stert
roasted	**gebakken**	gher**bah**kern
sautéed	**snel aangebraden**	snehl **aang**herbraadern
stewed	**gestoofd**	gher**stoaft**
underdone (rare)	**licht gebakken/rood**	likht gher**bah**kern/roat
medium	**net gaar gebakken**	neht ghaar gher**bah**kern
well-done	**doorgebakken**	**doar**gherbahkern

Meat specialities

Typical Dutch fare is very substantial and consists of a mix (*stamppot*—**stahm**pot) of vegetables and potatoes served with sausages and bacon.

Boerenkool met worst (boorern**koal** meht vorst) — curly kale and potatoes, served with smoked sausage; typical winter dish

Erwtensoep met kluif (**ehr**rternsoop meht klur^ewf) — thick pea soup with pieces of smoked sausage, cubes of pork fat, pig's knuckle and slices of pumpernickel (black rye bread); often served with brown bread

Hete bliksem (**hay**ter **blik**serm) — potatoes, bacon and apple, seasoned with butter, salt and sugar (the name means "hot lightning")

Hutspot met klapstuk (**hurt**spot meht **klahp**sturk) — potatoes, carrots and onions, often served with *klapstuk* (beef)

Jachtschotel (**yahkht**skhoaterl) — a casserole of meat, onions and potatoes, often served with apple sauce

Rolpens met rode kool (**rol**pehnss meht **roa**der koal) — fried slices of spiced and pickled minced beef and tripe, topped with a slice of apple and served with red cabbage

Zuurkool (**zewr**koal) — sauerkraut; often served with bacon or tender roast partridge

EATING OUT

Game and fowl

Chicken, duck and turkey are served in Dutch restaurants all through the year. For game proper you'll have to go to a special restaurant in the hunting areas (mainly in the east and south Netherlands). The hunting season runs from August/September to January/February. Ask the local tourist office for further details.

I'd like some game.	**Ik wil graag wild hebben.**	ik ✓il ghraakh ✓ilt **heh**bern
braadhaantje	**braat**haantyer	spring chicken
duif	dur[ew]f	pigeon
eend	aynt	duck
fazant	fah**zahnt**	pheasant
gans	gahnss	goose
gevogelte	ghe**voa**gherlter	fowl
haan	haan	cockerel
haas	haass	hare
hazepeper	**haa**zerpayperr	jugged hare
houtsnip	**ho[ow]t**snip	woodcock
kalkoen	kahl**koon**	turkey
kip	kip	chicken
gebraden kip	gher**braa**dern kip	roast chicken
konijn	koa**naiyn**	rabbit
korhoen	**kor**hoon	grouse
kuiken	**kur[ew]**kern	spring chicken
kwartel	**k✓ahr**terl	quail
parelhoen	**paa**rerlhoon	guinea fowl
patrijs	paa**traiyss**	partridge
reebout, reerug	**ray**bo[ow]t	venison
smient	smeent	widgeon
speenvarken	**spayn**vahrkern	suckling-pig
taling	**taa**ling	teal
watersnip	**✓aa**terrsnip	snipe
wild	✓ilt	game
wild zwijn	✓ilt z✓aiyn	wild boar

You usually have a choice of accompaniment to go with game:

brussels sprouts	**spruitjes**	**spru[ew]**tyerss
chestnut purée	**kastanjepuree**	kah**stahn**yerpewray
cranberry sauce	**vossebessen**	**vos**serbehsern
mashed potatoes	**aardappelpuree**	**aar**dahperlpewray

Vegetables

Fresh vegetables are available all year round, thanks to glasshouse cultivation. Large white asparagus, especially, is grown there, and you'll find it on the menu in May and June.

aardappelen	aardahperlern	potatoes
andijvie	ahn**daiy**vee	endive (Am. chicory)
artisjoken	ahr**tee**shokkern	artichoke
asperge(punten)	ahs**pehr**zher(**purn**tern)	asparagus (tips)
augurken	o^{ow}**ghurr**kern	gherkins
bieten	**bee**tern	beetroot
bloemkool	**bloom**koal	cauliflower
boerenkool	**boo**rernkoal	kale
bonen	**boa**nern	beans
witte bonen	**√it**ter **boa**nern	white beans
bruine bonen	**brur^{ew}**nern **boa**nern	kidney beans
Brussels lof	**brur**sserlss **lof**	chicory (Am. endive)
doperwtjes	**dop**ehrrtyerss	peas
eierplant	**aiy**yerrplahnt	aubergine (eggplant)
grauwe erwten	**ghro^{ow}**√er **ehrr**tern	chick-peas
groenten	**ghroon**tern	vegetables
gemengde groenten	gher**mehng**der **ghroon**tern	mixed vegetables
kappertjes	**kah**perrtyerss	capers
kapucijners	kahpew**saiyn**derrss	marrowfat peas
knolselderij	**knol**sehlderraiy	celeriac
komkommer	kom**kom**merr	cucumber
kool	koal	cabbage
rode kool	**roa**der koal	red cabbage
zuurkool	**zewr**koal	sauerkraut
kropsla	krop**slaa**	lettuce
linzen	**lin**zern	lentils
maïs	mah^{ee}ss	sweet corn
maïskolven	**mah^{ee}s**kolvern	corn on the cob
paddestoelen	**pah**derstoolern	mushrooms
peultjes	**purl**tyerss	sugar peas
pompoen (kleine)	pom**poon** (**klaiy**ner)	vegetable marrow (zucchini)
postelein	poster**laiyn**	purslane
prei	praiy	leeks
prinsessenbonen	prin**seh**sernboanern	green beans
radijs	raa**daiyss**	radishes
selderij	**sehl**derraiy	celery
sla	slaa	salad
snijbonen	**slaa**boanern	haricot beans
spinazie	speen**aa**zee	spinach

spruitjes	**sprur**^{ew}**tyerss**	brussels sprouts
tomaten	toa**maa**tern	tomatoes
tuinbonen	**tur**^{ew}**n**boanern	broad beans
uien	**ur**^{ew}yern	onions
venkel	**vehn**kerl	fennel
waterkers	**Vaa**terrkehrss	watercress
worteltjes	**Vor**terltyerss	carrots

And as a Dutch meal wouldn't be complete without potatoes, here are some ways of preparation:

aardappelpuree	aardahperlpewray	mashed potatoes
aardappelcroquetten	aardahperlkroakehtern	croquettes
gebakken	gher**bah**kern	fried
gekookt	gher**koakt**	boiled
in de schil gekookt	in der skhil gher**koakt**	boiled in their jackets
nieuwe aardappeltjes	**nee**^{oo}**Ver aardahperltyerss**	new potatoes
patates frites	paa**taht** freet	chips (french fries)

Some herbs commonly used in Dutch cooking:

basilicum	baa**zee**leekurm	basil
bieslook	**bees**loak	chive
bonenkruid	**boa**nernkrur^{ew}t	savory
dragon	draa**ghon**	tarragon
kervel	**kehr**verl	chervil
knoflook	**knof**loak	garlic
kruiden (gemengde)	**krur**^{ew}dern (gher**mehng**der)	herbs (mixed)
kruidnagel	**krur**^{ew}**tnaa**gherl	clove
mierikswortel	**mee**riks**Vor**terl	horseradish
marjolijn	mahryo**laiyn**	origan
nootmuskaat	noatmur**skaat**	nutmeg
peterselie	payterr**say**lee	parsley
rozemarijn	roazermaa**raiyn**	rosemary
tijm	taiym	thyme

You might also want:

mustard	**mosterd**	**mos**terrt
pepper	**peper**	**pay**perr
salad dressing	**slasaus**	**slaas**^{ow}ss
salt	**zout**	**zo**^{ow}t
sugar	**suiker**	**sur**^{ew}kerr

Sauces and preparations

The Dutch consume huge quantities of gravy (*saus*—so^{ow}ss or *jus*—zhew) and mayonnaise with their food. In the better restaurants you'll be served mainly French sauces. Below are brief descriptions of most sauces and garnishes you are likely to encounter.

Béarnaise saus	a creamy sauce flavoured with vinegar, egg yolks, white wine, shallots and tarragon
Béchamelsaus	a white sauce made of butter, flour and milk
Botersaus	a sauce made of butter, flour and fish stock
Bruine saus	butter, flour, stock, thyme, onions, parsley, cloves and bacon
Chaud-froid	gelatine, thick cream, egg yolks, mushrooms, onions and cloves
Gesmolten boter	melted butter, often served with fish
Hollandse saus (Sauce hollandaise)	egg yolks, butter and cream
Kaassaus	butter, flour, milk or stock and grated cheese
Kappertjessaus	butter, flour, stock, capers and vinegar
Madeirasaus	butter, flour, bacon, stock, cloves, thyme and Madeira
Mayonaise	egg yolks, oil, flavoured with vinegar or lemon juice
Mosselensaus	butter, flour, fish stock and mussels
Mosterdsaus	mustard added to a white sauce
Paprikasaus	butter, flour, stock, onion and paprika
Peterseliesaus	butter, flour, stock and parsley
Pikante saus	butter, flour, onions, vinegar, capers and white wine
Ravigottesaus	tarragon, chervil, chives, with stock and vinegar; served hot or cold
Speksaus	bacon, onions, flour, stock, flavoured with lemon juice
Tomatensaus	Tomatoes, onions, thyme and flour
Vinaigrettesaus	oil, vinegar, onion, parsley, gherkins and hard-boiled egg

Witte wijnsaus	butter, flour, stock, white wine and cream
Zure saus	butter sauce to which vinegar is added

Cheese

Although the round Edam cheese is better known abroad, many connoisseurs prefer Gouda, Leiden or cumin cheese. In Holland 26 different varieties of cheese are produced, including dessert cheeses such as the soft, creamy Kernhem. Generally speaking, it is not customary to eat cheese as a dessert except on rather special occasions. It is served either at breakfast and with a cold lunch, or in cubes together with ginger and pineapple chunks with an aperitif. Here are the names of some of the most popular cheeses:

Delftse kaas (**dehl**ftser kaass) **Leidse kaas** (laiytser kaass)	both these cheeses have the same flattened shape as Gouda cheese but they are made with cumin seeds; they are for this reason called *komijnekaas* (cumin cheese); less fatty than Edam and Gouda cheese.
Edammer kaas (ay**dah**merr kaass)	a firm round sphere; red on the outside (from Edam)
Friese Nagelkaas (freesser naagherlkaass)	made from skimmed milk and cloves (from Friesland)
Kernhemmer (**kehrn**hehmerr)	a successful effort to create a Dutch cheese of the soft dessert type; mellow in taste (from Kernhem)
Limburgse kaas (limburrghser kaass)	a creamy cheese with a spicy taste (from Limburg)
Witte meikaas (vitter maiykaass)	a creamy cheese with a high fat content; made from the first spring milk

Age is very important for Dutch cheeses. Young, fresh cheeses are called *jonge kaas* and the older ones *belegen kaas*. With age the taste becomes stronger and the texture firmer. If you like an aged cheese, ask for *oude* or *belegen kaas* (old cheese).

EATING OUT

Fruit

Do you have fresh fruit?	**Hebt u vers fruit?**	hehpt ew vehrss frurewt
I'd like a (fresh) fruit cocktail.	**Ik wil graag een (verse) vruchtensalade.**	ik √il ghraakh ayn (vehrser) vrurkhtern-saalaader

aardbeien	aartbaiyyern	strawberries
abrikozen	aabreekoazern	apricots
amandelen	aamahnderlern	almonds
ananas	ahnaanahss	pineapple
appel	ahperlss	apple
banaan	baanaan	banana
bosbessen	bosbehsern	blueberries/ bilberries
bramen	braamern	blackberries
citroen	seetroon	lemon
dadels	daaderlss	dates
druiven	drurewvern	grapes
frambozen	frahmboazern	raspberries
grapefruit	"grapefruit"	grapefruit
groene pruimen	ghrooner prurewmern	greengages
hazelnoten	haazerlnoatern	hazelnuts
kastanjes	kahstahnyerss	chestnuts
kersen	kehrsern	cherries
zwarte kersen	z√ahrter kehrsern	black cherries
kokosnoot	koakosnoat	coconut
kruisbessen	krurewsbehsern	gooseberries
mandarijn	mahndaaraiyn	tangerine
meloen	merloon	melon
noten	noatern	nuts
gemengde noten	ghermehngder noatern	mixed nuts
olijven	oalaiyvern	olives
peer	payr	pear
perzik	pehrzik	peach
pompelmoes	pomperlmooss	grapefruit
pruimen	prurewmern	plums
pruimedanten	prurewmerdahntern	prunes
rabarber	raabahrberr	rhubarb
rozijnen	roazaiynern	raisins
sinaasappel	seenaasahperlss	orange
vijgen	vaiyghern	figs
walnoten	√ahlnoatern	walnuts
watermeloen	√aaterrmerloon	watermelon

EATING OUT

Dessert

I'd like a dessert, please.	**Ik wil graag een nagerecht, alstublieft.**	ik vil ghraakh ayn **naa**gherrehkht ahlstew**bleeft**
What do you recommend?	**Wat beveelt u aan?**	vaht ber**vaylt** ew aan
Something light, please.	**Iets lichts, graag.**	eets likhts ghraakh
Just a small portion.	**Een kleine portie, alstublieft.**	ayn **klaiy**ner **por**see ahlstew**bleeft**
Nothing more, thank you.	**Niets meer, dank u.**	neets mayr dahnk ew

appelbeignets	**ah**perlbehñehss	apple fritters
appelgebak	**ah**perlgherbank	apple pastry
appeltaart	**ah**perltaart	apple tart
broodschoteltje	**broat**shoaterltyer	kind of bread pudding with apples, currants or raisins
Dame blanche	daam blahnsh	ice-cream with chocolate sauce
flensjes	**flehn**syerss	thin pancakes
met ananas	meht ahnaa**nahss**	with pineapple
fruit naar keuze	frur^{ew}t naar **kur**zer	a choice of fruit
gember met slagroom	**ghehm**berr meht **slahgh**roam	lumps of fresh ginger with whipped cream
ijs	aiyss	ice-cream
aardbeien	**aart**baiyyern	strawberry
chocolade	shokoa**laa**der	chocolate
pistache	pees**tahsh**	pistachio
vanille	vaa**nee**yer	vanilla
pannekoeken	**pah**nerkookern	pancakes
poffertjes	**po**fferrtyerss	small round fritter with butter and powder sugar
rijstebrijpudding	raiyster**braiy**purdding	rice pudding
schuimomelet	**skhur^{ew}**mommerleht	fluffy dessert omelet
slagroom	**slahgh**roam	whipped cream
vla	vlaa	custard
vlaai (Limburgse)	vlaa^{ee} (**lim**burrghser)	fruit tart
vruchtensla	**vrurkh**ternslaa	fruit salad
wentelteefjes	**vehn**terltayfyerss	fried slices of bread, dipped in egg batter and fried

The bill (check)

I'd like to pay.	**Ik wil graag afrekenen.**	ik ∀il ghraakh **ahf**raykernern
We'd like to pay separately.	**Wij willen graag apart afrekenen.**	∀aiy **∀**illern ghraakh aa**pahrt ahf**raykernern
You made a mistake in this bill, I think.	**Ik geloof, dat u een vergissing in de rekening gemaakt hebt.**	ik gher**loaf** daht ew ayn ver**ghiss**ing in der **ray**kerning gher**maakt** hehpt
What is this amount for?	**Voor wat is dit bedrag?**	voar ∀aht iss dit ber**drahkh**
Is service included?	**Is het inclusief bediening?**	iss heht inklew**seef** ber**dee**ning
Is everything included?	**Is alles inclusief?**	iss **ahl**erss inklew**seef**
Do you accept traveller's cheques?	**Neemt u reischeques aan?**	naymt ew **raiys**shehks aan
Thank you, this is for you.	**Dank u wel, dit is voor u.**	dahnk ew ∀ehl dit iss voar ew
Keep the change.	**Houdt u het wisselgeld maar.**	ho^{ow}t ew heht **∀**isserl-ghehlt maar
That was very good.	**Dat was erg lekker.**	daht ∀ahs ehrkh **leh**kerr
We enjoyed it, thank you.	**Wij hebben genoten, dank u wel.**	∀aiy **heh**bern gher**noa**tern dahnk ew ∀ehl

INCLUSIEF BEDIENING

SERVICE INCLUDED

Complaints

But perhaps you'll have something to complain about:

That is not what I ordered. I asked for ...	**Dat heb ik niet besteld. Ik heb ... gevraagd.**	daht hehp ik neet ber**stehlt**. ik hehp ... gher**vraakht**
May I change this?	**Kan ik wat anders krijgen?**	kahn ik ∀aht **ahn**derrss **kraiy**ghern

The meat is ...	**Het vlees is ...**	heht vlayss iss
overdone	**te gaar**	ter ghaar
underdone	**te rauw**	ter ro^{ow}ʋ
too rare	**te rood**	ter roat
too tough	**te taai**	ter taa^{ee}
This is too ...	**Dit is te ...**	dit iss ter
bitter/salty/sweet	**bitter/zout/zoet**	bitterr/zo^{ow}t/zoot
The food is cold.	**Het eten is koud.**	heht **ay**tern iss ko^{ow}t
This isn't fresh.	**Dit is niet vers.**	dit iss neet vehrss
What's taking you so long?	**Waarom duurt het zo lang?**	ʋaarom dewrt heht zoa lahng
Where are our drinks?	**Waar blijven onze drankjes?**	ʋaar **blaiy**vern onzer **drahn**kyerss
This isn't clean.	**Dit is vuil.**	dit iss vur^{ew}l
Would you ask the head waiter to come over?	**Wilt u de chefkelner vragen even hier te komen?**	ʋilt ew der **shehf**kehlnerr **vraa**ghern **ay**vern heer ter **koa**mern

Drinks

Aperitifs

Of all the alcoholic drinks, beer and jenever are the most favoured by the Dutch. The two best known local beers are *Amstel* and *Heineken.* If you want draught beer, just ask: *"Een pils van het vat, alstublieft"* (ayn pilss vahn heht vaht ahlstew**bleeft**).

There is also a kind of stout with a sweetish taste and a dark-brown colour, called *oud bruin*—o^{ow}t brur^{ew}n (old brown). Dutch jenever is mostly drunk as an aperitif. It is sometimes served with angostura or other bitters, in which case the *borreltje*—**bor**rerltyer (a glass of jenever) becomes a *bittertje*. In addition to old and young jenever, there are lemon-, red currant- and blackberry-flavoured jenevers.

I'd like a ...	**Ik wil graag ... hebben.**	ik ʋil ghraakh ... **heh**bern
glass of beer	**een biertje/een pils**	ayn **beer**tyer/ayn pilss
glass of jenever	**een borreltje**	ayn **bor**rerltyer

I'd like ... of ...	**Ik wil graag ...**	ik ∀il ghraakh
a carafe	**een karaf**	ayn kaa**rahf**
a bottle	**een fles**	ayn flehss
half a bottle	**een halve fles**	ayn **hahl**ver flehss
a glass	**een glas**	ayn ghlahss
a litre	**een liter**	ayn **lee**terr
I want a bottle of red/white wine.	**Ik wil een fles rode/witte wijn.**	ik ∀il ayn flehss **roa**der/**∀i**tter ∀aiyn

If you enjoyed the wine, you may want to say:

Please bring me another ...	**Wilt u mij nog een ... brengen, alstublieft?**	∀ilt ew maiy nokh ayn ... **brehn**gern ahlstew**bleeft**
Where does the wine come from?	**Waar komt de wijn vandaan?**	∀aar komt der ∀aiyn vahn**daan**

red	**rood**	roat
white	**wit**	∀it
rosé	**rosé**	roa**zay**
dry	**droog**	droakh
light	**licht**	likht
full-bodied	**vol**	vol
sparkling	**mousserend**	moos**say**rernt
very dry	**brut**	brewt
sweet	**zoet**	zoot

Other alcoholic drinks

In most restaurants, but especially in bars, you'll find a wide variety of cocktails or highballs. Names are generally the same as in English.

aperitif	**aperitief**	aapayree**teef**
beer	**bier**	beer
brandy	**brandewijn**	**brahn**der∀aiyn
gin-fizz	**gin-soda**	zhin **soa**daa
liqueur	**likeur**	lee**kurr**
Scotch	**Scotch whisky**	skotsh **∀is**kee
vodka	**wodka**	**∀ot**kaa

glass	**een glas**	ayn ghlahss
bottle	**een fles**	ayn flehss
neat (straight)	**zonder water**	zonderr **V**aaterr
on the rocks	**met ijsblokjes**	meht **aiys**blokyerss
with water	**met water**	meht **V**aaterr

Here are some typical Dutch drinks you may come across:

advokaat	ahtvoa**kaat**	a sort of egg-nog (egg liqueur); served with a small spoon
berenburg	**bay**rernburkh	Frisian gin
bessenjenever	**beh**ssernyernayverr	red currant-flavoured Dutch gin
bisschopswijn	**bis**skhops**V**aiyn	mulled claret (warm)
boerenjongens	boorern**yon**gernss	Dutch brandy with raisins
boerenmeisjes	boorern**maiy**sherss	Dutch brandy with apricots
jenever	yer**nay**verr	Dutch gin
jonge jenever	yonger yer**nay**verr	"young" Dutch gin
oude jenever	o^{ow}der yer**nay**verr	"old" Dutch gin
klare	**klaa**rer	common term for jenever
oranjebitter	oarah**ñer**bitterr	orange-flavoured bitters
pils	pilss	general name for beer

Dutch liqueurs are fairly reasonably priced.

Curaçao	kewraa**so^{ow}**	orange-flavoured liqueur
half om half	hahlf om hahlf	brownish liqueur with a sweet taste; rather strong
parfait d'amour	pahr**feh** daa**moor**	highly perfumed, amethyst-coloured
I'd like to try a glass of ..., please.	**Ik wil graag een glas ... proberen, alstublieft.**	ik **V**il ghraakh ayn ghlahss ... proa**bay**rern ahlstew**bleeft**

PROOST!
(proast)
CHEERS!

EATING OUT

Other beverages

buttermilk	**karnemelk**	**kahr**nermehlk
(hot) chocolate	**(warme) chocolademelk**	(**√ahr**mer) shoakoa**laa**dermehlk
coffee	**koffie**	**ko**ffee
cup of coffee	**een kopje koffie**	ayn **kop**yer **ko**ffee
coffee with cream	**koffie met room**	**ko**ffee meht roam
coffee with whipped cream	**koffie met slagroom**	**ko**ffee meht **slahgh**roam
espresso coffee	**een expresso**	ayn eks**prehs**soa
fruit juice	**vruchtesap**	**vrurkh**tersahp
lemonade	**limonade**	leemoa**naa**der
milk	**melk**	mehlk
mineral water	**mineraalwater**	meener**raal√aa**terr
squash	**kwast**	k√ahst
tea	**thee**	tay
with milk/lemon	**met melk/citroen**	meht mehlk/see**troon**
iced tea	**ijsthee**	**aiy**stay

Eating light—Snacks

bitterballen	**bi**tterr**bah**lern	small round breaded meatballs
belegde broodjes	ber**lehgh**der **broa**tyerss	sandwiches
broodje	**broa**tyer	roll
met ham	meht hahm	with ham
halfom	hahl**fom**	with liver and salted meat
met paling	meht **paa**ling	with smoked eel
met rookvlees	meht roak**vlays**	with smoked beef
knakworst	**knahk√**orst	hot smoked sausage
loempia	**loom**peeyaa	spring-roll; with vegetables and soya sprouts
pannekoek	**pah**nerkook	pancake
poffertjes	**po**fferrtyerss	small fritters
een zakje patates	ayn **zahk**yer paa**taht**	portion of chips (french fries)
met/zonder mayonaise	meht/**zon**derr maayoa**neh**zer	with/without mayonnaise
uitsmijter	**ur^{ew}t**smaiyterr	two slices of bread with ham, roast beef or cheese, topped by fried eggs

An excellent place to go for a snack is a *pannekoekhuisje* (pancake house) which may serve more than 50 different sorts of pancakes. Some have apple rings cooked in with them, others include currants, ginger or cheese. The most traditional one is *pannekoek met spek en stroop*—**pah**nerkook meht spehk ehn stroap (pancake with bacon and treacle [molasses]). Large towns sometimes have a *poffertjestent*, a stall which serves the delicious small round fritters called *poffertjes*—**po**fferrtyerss, laced with powder sugar and butter, all day long. Dutch children, especially, love them!

Indonesian dishes

As a result of many centuries of colonial presence in Indonesia (then called the Dutch East Indies), the Dutch have developed a real taste for spicy foods, and now consider Indonesian food part of Dutch cuisine. Here are some of the best known Indonesian specialities, including some adapted from Chinese cuisine, often found on the menu.

Bami goreng (baamee ghoarerng)	Chinese noodles with fried vegetables, diced pork, shrimp and shredded omelet
Kroepoek (kroopook)	a crisp, golden-brown shrimp wafer, often accompanying *rijsttafel*
Nassi goreng (nahssee ghoarerng)	fried rice with onions, meat, chicken, shrimp, ham and varied spices, usually topped with a fried egg
Nassi rames (nahssee raamehss)	a mini *rijsttafel*
Pisang goreng (peesahng ghoarerng)	fried banana, usually served with *rijsttafel*
Sajoer kerrie (saayoor kehree)	spicy cabbage soup; side dish to *rijsttafel*
Sambal goreng kering (sahmbahl ghoarerng kayring)	fried cabbage and ginger in coconut-milk sauce
Sateh babi (saatay baabee)	grilled cubes of pork on skewers; usually dipped in a hot peanut-butter sauce

The most famous Indonesian speciality is *rijsttafel*—(**raiyst**-taaferl) a real banquet of a meal. It consists of white rice served with an amazing number of small and very tasty dishes: stewed vegetables, delicately prepared beef and chicken, meat on skewers with peanut-butter sauce, fruits and spices, to name only a few. The spicy dishes can be extremely hot. Anything containing the word *sambal* will be peppery-hot; especially the tiny portions of *sambal oelek* and *sambal goreng*, that look like a ketchup paste, should be used sparingly.

Belgian (Flemish) specialities

Ballekesoep (**bah**lerkersoop)	a soup made from beef or chicken stock and onions, turnips, leeks and carrots; served with tiny meat-balls
Hochepot (**hosh**pot)	a casserole of beef, pork, mutton, carrots, cabbage, leeks, onions, potatoes and spices; garnished with fried sausages
Vlaamse bloedworst (**vlaam**ser **bloot**ʋorst)	black pudding served with apples
Vlaamse karbonade (**vlaam**ser kahrboa-**naa**der)	beef slices and onions braised in beer
Vlaamse kool (**vlaam**ser koal)	green cabbage prepared with apples and gooseberry jelly
Vlaamse hazepeper (**vlaam**ser **haa**zerpayperr)	jugged hare stewed with onions and plums
Waterzooi (**ʋaa**terrzoa^{ee})	chicken poached in white wine and shredded vegetables, cream and egg-yolk
Waterzooi met vis (**ʋaa**terrzoa^{ee} meht viss)	a delicious fish soup

Two somewhat special Belgian brews of beer you might like to try are *Kriekenlambiek* (**kree**kernlahmbeek), a strong Brussels bitter beer flavoured with morello cherries, and *trappistenbier* (trah**pis**ternbeer), a malt beer brewed originally by Trappist monks.

Travelling around

Plane

Holland is a small country and you are more likely to travel by car or train than by air. However, there are domestic flights between Amsterdam and Groningen, Enschede and Maastricht. In many tourist resorts, pleasure flights are operated all year round. The following expressions may therefore come in handy.

Is there a flight to Enschede?	**Is er een vlucht naar Enschede?**	iss ehr ayn vlurkht naar **ehns**kherday
When's the next plane to Amsterdam?	**Wanneer gaat het volgende vliegtuig naar Amsterdam?**	vahn**nayr** ghaat heht **vol**ghernder **vleegh**tur^{ew}kh naar ahmsterr**dahm**
Can I make a connection to Maastricht?	**Heb ik aansluiting naar Maastricht?**	hehp ik **aan**slur^{ew}ting naar maas**trikht**
I'd like a ticket to Brussels.	**Ik wil graag een vliegbiljet naar Brussel.**	ik vil ghraakh ayn **vleegh**bilyeht naar **brur**sserl
What's the fare to Groningen?	**Hoeveel kost een vlucht naar Groningen?**	hoo**vayl** kost ayn vlurkht naar **ghroa**ningern
single (one-way)	**enkele reis**	**ehn**kerler raiyss
return (round trip)	**retour**	rer**toor**
What time does the plane take off?	**Hoe laat vertrekt het vliegtuig?**	hoo laat verr**trehkt** heht **vleegh**tur^{ew}kh
What time do I have to check in?	**Hoe laat moet ik mij melden?**	hoo laat moot ik maiy **mehl**dern
What's the flight number?	**Wat is het vluchtnummer?**	vaht iss heht **vlurkht**nurmerr
What time do we arrive?	**Hoe laat komen wij aan?**	hoo laat **koa**mern vaiy aan
Is there a duty-free shop?	**Is er een duty-free winkel?**	iss ehr ayn "duty-free" **vin**kerl

AANKOMST
ARRIVAL

VERTREK
DEPARTURE

Train

Due to its geographical location, a dense rail network and short distances, Holland lends itself very well to sightseeing by train. Season tickets entitle the holder to unlimited travel on the entire Dutch railway system. There are one-day, eight-day, weekend and monthly season tickets. For further information apply to the railway stations or the VVV offices.

TEE-trein (tay ay ay traiyn)	Trans-Europ-Express; a luxury international service with first class only; supplementary fare and advance booking required.
D-trein (day traiyn)	Through train, often connecting with an international train. Seat reservation advisable.
Auto-slaaptrein (o^{ow}toa **slaap**traiyn)	Car train. Put your car aboard and take a rest.
Intercity (interr**sitee**)	Fast train stopping only at a few stations.
Sneltrein (**snehl**traiyn)	Long-distance express stopping only at main stations.
Stoptrein (**stop**traiyn)	Local train stopping at all stations.
Boottrein (**boat**traiyn)	Boat train connecting with the ferry crossing to England.

ROKEN
SMOKERS

ROKEN VERBODEN
NON SMOKERS

Slaapwagen (**slaap**ʋaaghern)	Sleeping-car with individual compartments (single or double) and washing facilities.
Couchette (koo**sheht**)	Berth with blankets and pillows. An ordinary compartment can be transformed into six berths.
Restauratiewagen (rehstoa**raatsee**-ʋaaghern)	Dining-car.
Bagagewagen (baa**ghaa**zher-ʋaaghern)	Guard's van (baggage car); normally only registered luggage permitted.

To the railway station

Where's the railway station?	**Waar is het station?**	√aar iss heht stahts**yon**
Taxi, please!	**Taxi, alstublieft!**	**tahk**see ahlstew**bleeft**
Take me to the railway station.	**Naar het station, alstublieft.**	naar heht stahts**yon** ahlstew**bleeft**
What's the fare?	**Hoeveel ben ik u schuldig?**	hoo**vayl** behn ik ew **skhurl**derkh

INGANG	ENTRANCE
UITGANG	EXIT
NAAR DE PERRONS	PLATFORMS (TRACKS)

Where's the...?

Where is/are the ...?	**Waar is/zijn ...?**	√aar iss/zaiyn
accommodation bureau	**het huisvestingbureau**	heht **hur^{ew}**svehstingbewroa
booking office	**het plaatsbureau**	heht **plaats**bewroa
currency-exchange office	**het wisselkantoor**	heht **√**isserlkahntoar
florist's	**de bloemist**	der bloo**mist**
information	**het inlichtingenbureau**	heht **in**likhtingernbewroa
left luggage office (baggage check)	**het bagagedepot**	heht baa**ghaa**zherdehpoat
letter box	**de brievenbus**	der **bree**vernburss
lost-property (lost and found) office	**het bureau voor gevonden voorwerpen**	heht bew**roa** voar gher**von**dern **voar√**ehrpern
luggage lockers	**de bagagekluizen**	der baa**ghaa**zherklur^{ew}zern
news-stand	**de kiosk**	der kee**yosk**
platform 7	**perron 7**	peh**rron** 7
reservations office	**het bespreekbureau**	heht ber**spraykbewroa**
restaurant	**het restaurant**	heht rehstoa**rahnt**
snack bar	**de snackbar**	der "snackbar"
ticket office	**het loket**	heht loa**keht**
track 7	**spoor 7**	spoar **zay**vern
waiting-room	**de wachtkamer**	der **√ahkht**kaamerr
Where are the toilets?	**Waar zijn de toiletten?**	√aar zaiyn der t**√aaleh**tern

FOR TAXI, see page 27

Inquiries

In Holland and Belgium **i** means information office.

When is the ... train to The Hague?	**Wanneer gaat de ... trein naar Den Haag?**	**ʋahnayr** ghaat der ... traiyn naar dehn haakh
first/last/next	**eerste/laatste/ volgende**	**ayr**ster/**laat**ster/ **vol**ghernder
What time does the train for Utrecht leave?	**Hoe laat vertrekt de trein naar Utrecht?**	hoo laat verr**trehkt** der traiyn naar **ewt**rehkht
What's the fare to Haarlem?	**Hoeveel kost een kaartje naar Haarlem?**	hoo**vayl** kost ayn **kaar**tyer naar **haar**lehm
Is it a through train?	**Is het een doorgaande trein?**	iss heht ayn **doar**ghaander traiyn
Will the train leave on time?	**Vertrekt de trein op tijd?**	verr**trehkt** der traiyn op taiyt
What time does the train arrive at Rotterdam?	**Hoe laat komt de trein in Rotterdam aan?**	hoo laat komt der traiyn in rotterr**dahm** aan
Is there a dining-car on the train?	**Is er een restauratiewagen in de trein?**	iss ehr ayn rehstoa**raat**see-ʋaaghern in der traiyn
Is there a sleeping-car on the train?	**Is er een slaapwagen in de trein?**	iss ehr ayn **slaap**ʋaaghern in der traiyn
Does the train stop at Groningen?	**Stopt de trein in Groningen?**	stopt der traiyn in **ghroa**ningern
What platform does the train from Gouda arrive at?	**Op welk perron komt de trein uit Gouda aan?**	op ʋehlk peh**rron** komt der traiyn ur^{ew}t **gho**^{ow}daa aan
What platform does the train for Brussels leave from?	**Van welk perron vertrekt de trein naar Brussel?**	vahn ʋehlk peh**rron** verr**trehkt** der traiyn naar **brur**sserl
I'd like to buy a timetable.	**Ik wil graag een spoorboekje hebben.**	ik ʋil ghraakh ayn **spoar**bookyer **heh**bern

INLICHTINGEN	INFORMATION
WISSELKANTOOR	CURRENCY EXCHANGE

Het is een doorgaande trein.	It's a through train.
U moet overstappen in...	You have to change in...
Stapt u in ... over en neemt u dan een stoptrein.	Change at ... and get a local train.
Perron 7 is...	Platform 7 is...
daar/boven	over there/upstairs
aan uw linkerhand/rechterhand	on the left/right
Om ... is een trein naar ...	There's a train to ... at ...
Uw trein vertrekt van perron 8.	Your train will leave from platform 8.
Er is een vertraging van ... minuten.	There'll be a delay of... minutes.

Tickets

I want a ticket to Alkmaar.	**Ik wil graag een ... naar Alkmaar hebben.**	ik ʋil ghraakh ayn ... naar **ahlk**maar **heh**bern
single (one-way)	**enkele reis**	**ehn**kerler raiyss
return (roundtrip)	**retourtje**	rer**toor**tyer
first/second class	**kaartje eerste/ tweede klas**	**kaar**tyer **ayr**ster/ **tʋay**der klahss
Isn't it half price for the child?*	**Betaalt men voor kinderen niet halve prijs?**	ber**taalt** mehn voar **kin**derrern neet **hahl**ver praiyss
He/She is 8.	**Hij/Zij is 8.**	haiy/zaiy iss 8

Eerste of tweede klas?	First or second class?
Een enkele reis of een retourtje?	Single or return (one-way or roundtrip)?
Hoe oud is hij/zij?	How old is he/she?

* In Holland children between 4 and 9 years of age travel half fare; in Belgium, between 4 and 12.

FOR NUMBERS, see page 175

All aboard

Is this the right platform for the train to Paris?	**Is dit het goeie perron voor de trein naar Parijs?**	iss dit heht **goo**yer peh**rron** voar der traiyn naar paa**raiyss**
Is this the right train to Antwerp?	**Is dit de trein naar Antwerpen?**	iss dit der traiyn naar **ahnt**ꝟehrpern
Excuse me. May I get by?	**Neemt u mij niet kwalijk, mag ik er even langs?**	naymt ew maiy neet **kꝞaa**lerk mahkh ik ehr **ay**vern lahngss
Is this seat taken?	**Is deze plaats bezet?**	iss **day**zer plaats ber**zeht**
I think that's my seat.	**Ik geloof dat dit mijn plaats is.**	ik gher**loaf** daht dit maiyn plaats iss
Would you let me know before we get to Arnhem?	**Wilt u mij waarschuwen voordat wij in Arnhem aankomen?**	ꝟilt ew maiy **ꝟaar**skhewꝟern **voar**daht ꝟaiy in **ahrn**hehm **aan**koamern
What station is this?	**Welk station is dit?**	ꝟehlk staht**syon** iss dit
How long does the train stop here?	**Hoe lang stopt de trein hier?**	hoo lahng stopt der traiyn heer
When do we get to The Hague?	**Wanneer komen wij in Den Haag aan?**	ꝟah**nayr koa**mern ꝟaiy in dehn haakh aan

Sometime on the journey the ticket collector (*de conducteur*—der kondurk**turr**) will come around and say: *Uw kaartjes, alstublieft!* (Tickets, please!)

Eating

If you want a full meal in the dining-car, you may have to get a ticket from the attendant who will come round to your compartment. There are usually two sittings each for breakfast, lunch and dinner.

You can get snacks and drinks in the buffet-car and in the dining-car when it's not being used for main meals. On some trains an attendant comes around with snacks, coffee, tea and soft drinks. At the larger stations there are refreshment carts.

First/Second call for dinner!	**Eerste/Tweede bediening!**	ayrster/**tʋay**der ber**dee**ning
Where's the dining-car?	**Waar is de restauratiewagen?**	ʋaar iss der rehstoa**raat**seeʋaaghern

Sleeping

Are there any free compartments in the sleeping-car?	**Zijn er nog slaapcoupés vrij?**	zaiyn ehr nokh **slaap**koopayss vraiy
Where's the sleeping-car/couchette-car?	**Waar is de slaapwagen/de couchettewagen?**	ʋaar iss der **slaap**ʋaaghern/der koo**sheh**terʋaaghern
Where's my berth?	**Waar is mijn couchette?**	ʋaar iss maiyn koo**sheh**ter
Compartments 18 and 19, please.	**Coupé 18 en 19, alstublieft.**	koo**pay** 18 ehn 19 ahlstew**bleeft**
I'd like a lower berth.	**Ik wil graag een couchette beneden.**	ik ʋil ghraakh ayn koo**sheh**ter ber**nay**dern
Would you make up our berths?	**Wilt u onze couchettes gereedmaken?**	ʋilt ew **on**zer koo**sheh**terss gher**rayt**maakern
Would you call me at 7 o'clock?	**Wilt u mij om 7 uur wekken?**	ʋilt ew maiy om 7 ewr **ʋeh**kern
Would you bring me some coffee in the morning?	**Wilt u mij morgenochtend een kopje koffie brengen?**	ʋilt ew maiy morghern**okh**ternt ayn **kop**yer koffee **brehng**ern

Baggage—Porters

Porter!	**Kruier, alstublieft!**	**krur**^{ew}yerr ahlstew**bleeft**
Can you help me with with my bags?	**Kunt u mij met mijn bagage helpen?**	kurnt ew maiy meht maiyn baa**ghaa**zher **hehl**pern
Can I register these bags?	**Kan ik deze koffers ter verzending aangeven?**	kahn ik **day**zer **kof**ferrss tehr verr**zehn**ding aan**gay**vern

FOR PORTERS, see also page 24

Lost property

Where's the lost-property (lost and found) office?	**Waar is het bureau voor gevonden voorwerpen?**	Vaar iss heht bew**roa** voar gher**vondern voar**-Vehrpern
I've lost my...	**Ik heb mijn ... verloren.**	ik hehp maiyn... verr**loa**rern
handbag	**handtas**	**hahnt**tahss
passport	**paspoort**	**pahs**poart
ticket	**biljet**	bil**yeht**
wallet	**portefeuille**	porter**fur**^{ew}yer
I lost it in...	**Ik heb het in ... verloren.**	ik hehp heht in ... verr**loa**rern
It's very valuable.	**Het is heel kostbaar.**	heht iss hayl **kost**baar

Underground (subway)

The nature of the subsoil in Holland long made the construction of an underground impossible. However, Amsterdam and Rotterdam do now have their subways *(metro)*. The complete underground/overground run will eventually link Amsterdam's Central Station with Schiphol Airport and The Hague.

Where's the nearest metro station?	**Waar is het dichtst-bijzijnde metro-station?**	Vaar iss heht dikhtst-baiy**zaiyn**der **may**troa-stahts**yon**

Ferry services and tolls

With so much water around, ferries still have a real function in Holland. Many ferry services can be found on secondary roads crossing rivers and canals. Most ferries are equipped to carry motor vehicles and their fares are reasonable. Delays may occur, especially when there is fog. In certain cases tolls are charged for bridges, dams and tunnels.

What time does the next ferryboat cross?	**Hoe laat vertrekt de volgende veerboot?**	hoo laat verr**trehkt** der **vol**ghernder **vayr**boat
How much is the toll fee?	**Hoeveel tol moet ik betalen?**	hoo**vayl** tol moot ik ber**taa**lern

Bus—Tram (streetcar)

Public transport in the cities is provided mainly by buses and trams. Between cities and smaller towns and villages, there are regular bus services. Many bus companies have cheap day tickets for their whole system. VVV offices will supply you with the necessary information on departure times and fares. Some cities have introduced an automatic system of paying the fare, whereby you insert the exact change into a ticket dispenser at the bus stop or have the machine validate your prepaid ticket.

Where's the nearest bus/tram stop?	**Waar is de dichtstbijzijnde bus-/tramhalte?**	ꝟaar iss der dikhtst-baiy**zaiy**nder **burss**-/**trehm**hahlter
I'd like a booklet of tickets.	**I wil graag een rittenkaart, alstublieft.**	ik ꝟil ghraakh ayn **burss**ritternkaart ahlstew**bleeft**
Where can I get a bus/tram to the town centre?	**Waar kan ik een bus/tram naar het centrum nemen?**	ꝟaar kahn ik ayn burss trehm/naar heht **sehn**trurm **nay**mern
What bus do I take for the Central Museum?	**Welke bus moet ik naar het Centraal Museum nemen?**	Ꝟ**ehl**ker burss moot ik naar heht sehn**traal** mew**zay**yurm **nay**mern

BUSHALTE	REGULAR BUS STOP
STOPT OP VERZOEK	STOPS ON REQUEST

When is the ... bus to the Rokin?	**Wanneer gaat de ... bus naar het Rokin?**	ꝟah**nayr** ghaat der ... burss naar heht roa**kin**
first/last/next	**eerste/laatste/ volgende**	**ayr**ster/**laat**ster/ **vol**ghernder
How often do the buses to the zoo run?	**Hoe vaak gaan de bussen naar de dierentuin?**	hoo vaak ghaan der **burss**ern naar der **dee**rernturewn
How much is the fare to ...	**Wat kost een kaartje naar ...?**	ꝟaht kost ayn **kaar**tyer naar
Do I have to change buses?	**Moet ik overstappen?**	moot ik oaverr**stah**pern
How long does the journey take?	**Hoelang duurt de reis?**	hoo**lahng** dewrt der raiyss

Other modes of transport

Bicycles and mopeds are extremely popular in Holland. A well-developed system of cycle tracks and trails throughout the country may encourage many people to tour Holland by bike. Bikes can be hired from bicycle shops or at railway stations. Prices vary and will depend on the duration of the contract and the quality of the bike.

You may find yourself trying any one of these types of vehicles to get around:

barge	**schuit**	skhur^{ew}t
bicycle	**fiets**	feets
boat	**boot**	boat
canoe	**kano**	kaanoa
motorboat	**motorboot**	moaterrboat
rowing-boat	**roeiboot**	roo^{ee}boat
sailing-boat	**zeilboot**	zaiylboat
car	**auto**	o^{ow}toa
hovercraft	**glijboot**	ghlaiyboat
moped	**bromfiets**	bromfeets
motorcycle	**motorfiets**	moaterrfeets
paddle-wheel steamer	**raderstoomboot**	raadehrstoamboat

Or perhaps you prefer:

hitchhiking	**liften**	liftern
horse-riding	**paardrijden**	paartraiydern
walking	**lopen**	loapern

The Dutch are enthusiastic walkers, and all year round walking tours through woodland and heath as well as on the beaches and through the dunes are organized. If you wish to participate in one of these walking events, go to a VVV office for information.

Around and about—Sightseeing

In this section we are more concerned with the cultural aspects of town life. For entertainment see page 80.

Can you recommend a good guide book on Amsterdam?	**Kunt u mij een goede reisgids voor Amsterdam aanbevelen?**	kurnt ew maiy ayn **ghoo**der **raiys**ghits voar ahmster**dahm aan**bervaylern
Is there a tourist office?	**Is er een VVV?**	iss ehr heer ayn vayvayvay
Where's the tourist office?	**Waar is de VVV?**	ꝟaar iss der vayvayvay
What are the main points of interest?	**Wat zijn de belangrijkste bezienswaardigheden?**	ꝟaht zaiyn der ber**lahng**raiykster berzeenss**ꝟaar**derghhaydern
We're here for...	**Wij blijven hier maar...**	ꝟaiy **blaiy**vern heer maar
only a few hours	**een paar uur**	ayn paar ewr
a day	**een dag**	ayn dahkh
3 days	**3 dagen**	3 **daa**ghern
a week	**een week**	ayn ꝟayk
Can you recommend a sightseeing tour?	**Kunt u mij een rondleiding aanbevelen?**	kurnt ew maiy ayn **ront**laiyding **aan**bervaylern
Where does the bus start from?	**Van waar vertrekt de bus?**	vahn ꝟaar verr**trehkt** der burss
Will it pick us up at the hotel?	**Haalt hij ons van het hotel af?**	haalt haiy onss vahn heht hoa**tehl** af
Where's the nearest point of departure for canal boat trips?	**Waar is het dichtstbijzijnde vertrekpunt voor een rondvaart op de grachten?**	ꝟaar iss heht dikhtst**baiyzaiy**nder verr**trehk**purnt voar ayn **ront**vaart op der **ghrahkh**tern
What bus/tram (streetcar) do we take?	**Welke bus/tram moeten we nemen?**	**ꝟehl**ker burss/trehm mootern ꝟer **nay**mern
How much does the tour cost?	**Wat kost de rondleiding?**	ꝟaht kost der **ront**laiyding
What time does the tour start?	**Hoe laat begint de rondleiding?**	hoo laat ber**ghint** der **ront**laiyding

FOR TIME OF DAY, see page 178

We'd like to hire a car for the day.	**Wij willen graag voor vandaag een auto huren.**	ʋaiy ʋillern ghraakh voar vahn**daakh** ayn o^{ow}toa **hew**rern
Is there an English speaking guide?	**Is er een gids die Engels spreekt?**	iss ehr ayn ghits dee **ehng**erlss spraykt
Where is/are the ...?	**Waar is/zijn ...?**	ʋaar iss/zaiyn
abbey	**de abdij**	der ap**daiy**
airport	**het vliegveld**	heht **vleegh**vehlt
aquarium	**het aquarium**	heht aak**ʋaa**reeyurm
art gallery	**het museum voor beeldende kunst**	heht mew**zay**urm voar **bayl**dernder kurnst
artists' quarter	**de artiestenbuurt**	der ahr**tees**ternbewrt
botanical gardens	**de botanische tuinen**	der boa**taa**neesser **tur^{ew}**nern
business district	**de zakenwijk**	der **zaa**kernʋaiyk
canal	**de gracht**	der ghrahkht
castle	**het kasteel**	heht kahs**tayl**
cathedral	**de kathedraal**	der kahter**draal**
cave	**de grot**	der ghrot
cemetery	**het kerkhof**	heht **kehrk**hof
chapel	**de kapel**	der kaa**pehl**
church	**de kerk**	der kehrk
city centre	**het stadscentrum**	heht **stahts**sehntrurm
city hall	**het stadhuis**	heht staht**hur^{ew}ss**
concert hall	**het concertgebouw**	heht kon**sehrt**gherbo^{ow}
convent	**het klooster**	heht **kloa**sterr
docks	**de dokhavens**	der **dok**haaverns
downtown area	**het stadscentrum**	heht **stahts**sehntrurm
exhibition	**de tentoonstelling**	der tehn**toan**stehling
fortress	**het fort**	heht fort
fountain	**de fontein**	der fon**taiyn**
gardens	**het park**	heht pahrk
harbour	**de haven**	der **haa**vern
lake	**het meer**	heht mayr
market	**de markt**	der mahrkt
memorial	**het gedenkteken**	heht gher**dehnk**taykern
monastery	**het klooster**	heht **kloa**sterr
monument	**het monument**	heht moanew**mehnt**
museum	**het museum**	heht mew**zay**yurm
observatory	**het observatorium**	heht opsehrvaa**toa**reeyurm
old town	**het oude stadscentrum**	heht **o^{ow}**der **stahts**sehntrurm
opera house	**de opera**	der **oa**perraa
palace	**het paleis**	heht paa**laiyss**
park	**het park**	heht pahrk

parliament building	**het parlements-gebouw**	heht pahrler**mehnts**-gherbo^{ow}
planetarium	**het planetarium**	heht plaaner**taa**reeyurm
post office	**het postkantoor**	heht **post**kahntoar
ruins	**de ruines**	der rew**ʋee**nerss
shopping centre	**de winkelwijk**	der **ʋ**inkerlʋaiyk
stadium	**het stadion**	heht staadee**yon**
statue	**het standbeeld**	heht **stahnt**baylt
stock exchange	**de beurs**	der burrss
supreme court	**het Hooggerechts-hof**	heht hoaghgher**rehkhts**hof
theatre	**de schouwburg**	der **skho**^{ow}burrkh
tomb	**het graf**	heht ghrahf
tower	**de toren**	der **toa**rern
town hall	**het stadhuis**	heht staht**hur**^{ew}**ss**
windmill	**de windmolen**	der **ʋint**moalern
zoo	**de dierentuin**	der **dee**rerntur^{ew}n

Admission

Is ... open on Sundays?	**Is ... open op zondag?**	iss ... **oa**pern op **zon**dahkh
When does it open/close?	**Wanneer gaat het open/dicht?**	ʋahn**nayr** ghaat heht **oa**pern/dikht
How much is the entrance fee?	**Hoeveel is de toe-gangsprijs?**	hoo**vayl** kost der **too**ghahngspraiyss
Is there any reduc-tion for...?	**Is er reduktie voor...?**	iss ehr rer**durk**see voar
children	**kinderen**	**kin**derrern
pensioners	**gepensioneerden**	gherpehnsyoa**nayr**dern
students	**studenten**	stew**dehn**tern
Can I buy a catalogue?	**Mag ik een katalo-gus van u?**	mahgh ik ayn kaa**taa**loaghurss vahn ew
Have you a guide book in English?	**Hebt u een gids in het Engels?**	hehpt ew ayn ghits in heht **ehn**gerlss
Is it all right to take pictures?	**Mag je hier foto's nemen?**	mahgh yer heer **foa**toass **nay**mern

VRIJE TOEGANG	ADMISSION FREE
VERBODEN TE FOTOGRAFEREN	NO CAMERAS ALLOWED

Who—What—When?

What's that building?	**Wat is dat voor een gebouw?**	ꝟaht iss daht voar ayn gher**bo^{ow}**
Who was the…	**Wie was…?**	ꝟee ꝟahss
architect	**de architekt**	der ahrkhee**tehkt**
artist	**de artiest**	der ahr**teest**
painter	**de schilder**	der **skhil**derr
sculptor	**de beeldhouwer**	der **baylt**ho^{ow}err
Who built it?	**Wie heeft het gebouwd?**	ꝟee hayft heht gher**bo^{ow}t**
When was it built?	**Wanneer is het gebouwd?**	ꝟah**nayr** iss heht gher**bo^{ow}t**
Who painted that picture?	**Wie heeft dat schilderij gemaakt?**	ꝟee hayft daht skhilderr**aiy** gher**maakt**
When did he live?	**Wanneer leefde hij?**	ꝟah**nayr layf**der haiy
Where's the house where … lived?	**Waar is het huis waar … gewoond heeft?**	ꝟaar iss heht hur^{ew}ss ꝟaar … gher**woant** hayft
We're/I'm interested in…	**Wij hebben/Ik heb belangstelling voor…**	ꝟaiy **heh**bern/ik hehp ber**lahng**stehling voar
antiques	**antiek**	ahn**teek**
applied art	**kunstnijverheid**	**kurnst**naiyverrhaiyt
archaeology	**archeologie**	ahrkhayoaloa**ghee**
art	**kunst**	kurnst
botany	**plantkunde**	**plahnt**kurnder
ceramics	**ceramiek**	sayraa**meek**
coins	**munten**	**murn**tern
crafts	**ambachten**	**ahm**bahkhtern
fine arts	**beeldende kunst**	**bayl**dernder kurnst
furniture	**meubelen**	**mur**berlern
geology	**geologie**	ghayoaloa**ghee**
medicine	**geneeskunde**	gher**nays**kurnder
music	**muziek**	mew**zeek**
natural history	**natuurlijke historie**	naa**tewr**lerker hi**stoa**ree
ornithology	**vogelkunde**	**voa**gherlkurnder
painting	**schilderkunst**	**skhil**derrkurnder
pottery	**pottenbakkerij**	potternbahkker**raiy**
sculpture	**beeldhouwkunst**	**baylt**ho^{ow}kurnst
zoology	**dierkunde**	**deer**kurnder
Where's the … department?	**Waar is de … afdeling?**	ꝟaar iss der … **ahf**dayling

Just the adjective you've been looking for ...

It's...	**Het is...**	heht iss
amazing	**verbazingwekkend**	verrbaazing**√eh**kernt
awful	**afschuwelijk**	ahf**skhew**√erlerk
beautiful	**mooi**	moa[ee]
gloomy	**somber**	**som**berr
impressive	**indrukwekkend**	indrurk**√eh**kernt
interesting	**interessant**	interreh**ssahnt**
magnificent	**geweldig**	gher**√ehl**dikh
overwhelming	**overweldigend**	oaverr**√ehl**derghernt
strange	**vreemd**	vraymt
superb	**prachtig**	**prahkh**terkh
terrible	**vreselijk**	**vray**serlerk
terrifying	**angstaanjagend**	ahngstaan**yaa**ghernt
tremendous	**enorm**	ay**norm**
ugly	**lelijk**	**lay**lerk

Religious services

Three-quarters of Holland's population is more or less equally divided into Catholics and Protestants (the remaining one-fourth is non-denominational). A number of other religions are also represented. Most churches are only open during the services. If you want to visit a church, apply to the sexton (*koster*—**kos**terr).

Is there a ... near here?	**Is er een ... in de buurt?**	iss ehr ayn ... in der bewrt
Catholic church	**Katholieke kerk**	kahtoa**lee**ker kehrk
Protestant church	**Protestantse kerk**	proatehs**tahnt**ser kehrk
synagogue	**Synagoge**	seenaa**ghoa**gher
At what time is...?	**Hoe laat begint de...?**	hoo laat ber**ghint** der
mass/the service	**hoogmis/dienst**	**hoagh**miss/deenst
Where can I find a ... who speaks English?	**Waar kan ik een... vinden die Engels spreekt?**	√aar kahn ik ayn **vin**dern dee **ehng**erlss spraykt
minister	**dominee**	**doa**meenay
priest	**priester**	**pree**sterr
rabbi	**rabbi**	**rah**bee

Relaxing

Cinema (movies)—Theatre

Film showings in Holland are seldom continuous. Seats can generally be reserved in advance. The programme usually consists of one feature film, a short documentary or newsreel and numerous advertisements. There is an intermission during the feature. The first performance starts at about 2 p.m., the last at about 10 p.m. Late-night shows on Saturdays are found mainly in the large cities. Cinemas always show films in the original language with subtitles in Dutch.

Dutch theatres close one day a week. You can find out what is playing from newspapers or from the local tourist office (VVV). In the larger places there are publications of the type "This week in...", and the VVV offices there have a theatre booking office. It is advisable to book in advance.

There is an *Informaphone* in the VVV office in front of Amsterdam's Central Station which will tell you (in English) what's on in Amsterdam. The people in the tourist office will tell you how to use the phone.

Have you a copy of "This week in..."?	**Mag ik een exemplaar van „Deze week in..." van u?**	mahkh ik ayn ehksehm**plaar** vahn **day**zer ∀ayk in ... vahn ew
What's showing at the cinema tonight?	**Wat draait er vanavond in de bioscoop?**	∀aht draa^{ee}t ehr vahn-aavont in der beeyos**koap**
Where's that new film by ... being shown?	**Waar draait die nieuwe film van...?**	∀aar draa^{ee}t dee nee^{oo}∀er film vahn
What's playing at the ... Theatre?	**Wat wordt er in de ... schouwburg gespeeld?**	∀aht ∀ort ehr in der ... skho^{ow}burrkh gher**spaylt**
What sort of play is it?	**Wat voor een toneelstuk is het?**	∀aht voar ayn toa**nayl**sturk iss heht

Who's the playwright?	**Wie is de schrijver?**	ꝟee iss der **skhraiy**verr
Can you recommend a...?	**Kunt u mij ... aanbevelen?**	kurnt ew maiy aanber**vay**lern
comedy	**een blijspel**	ayn **blaiy**spehl
good film	**een goede film**	ayn **ghoo**der film
something light	**iets luchtigs**	eets **lurkh**terkhs
musical	**een musical**	ayn "musical"
play	**een toneelstuk**	ayn toa**nayl**sturk
revue	**een revue**	ayn rer**vew**
thriller	**een sensatiestuk**	ayn sehn**saat**seesturk
western	**een western**	ayn **ꝟeh**sterrn
At what theatre is that new play by ... being performed?	**In welke schouwburg speelt dat nieuwe stuk van ...?**	in **ꝟehl**ker **skho^{ow}**burrkh spaylt daht **nee^{oo}**ꝟer sturk vahn
Who's in it?	**Wie spelen er in?**	ꝟee **spay**lern ehr in
Who's playing the lead?	**Wie speelt de hoofdrol?**	ꝟee spaylt der **hoaf**trol
Who's the director?	**Wie is de regisseur?**	ꝟee iss der rayghee**ssurr**
What time does it begin?	**Hoe laat begint het?**	hoo laat ber**ghint** heht
What time does the show end?	**Hoe laat is de voorstelling afgelopen?**	hoo laat iss der **voar**stehling **ahf**gherloapern
Are there any tickets for tonight?	**Zijn er nog plaatsen voor vanavond?**	zaiyn ehr nokh **plaat**sern voar vahn**aa**vont
I want to reserve 2 tickets for the show on Friday evening.	**Ik wil graag 2 plaatsen bespreken voor de voorstelling van vrijdagavond.**	ik ꝟil ghraakh 2 **plaat**sen ber**spray**kern voar der **voar**stehling vahn **vraiy**dahkhaavont
Can I have a ticket for the matinée on Tuesday?	**Ik wil graag één plaats voor de middagvoorstelling op dinsdag.**	ik ꝟil ghraakh ayn plaats voar der **mid**dahghvoarstehling op **dins**dahkh
I want a seat in the stalls (orchestra)/circle (mezzanine).	**Ik wil graag een plaats in de stalles/op het balkon.**	ik ꝟil ghraakh ayn plaats in der **stah**lerss op heht bahl**kon**
How much are the front-row seats?	**Wat kosten de plaatsen op de eerste rij?**	ꝟaht **kos**tern der **plaat**sern op der **ayr**ster raiy
Not too far back.	**Niet te ver naar achteren.**	neet ter vehr naar **ahkh**terrern

May I please have a programme?	**Mag ik een programma, alstublieft?**	mahkh ik ayn proa**ghrah**maa ahlstew**bleeft**
Where's the cloakroom?	**Waar is de vestiaire?**	ʋaar iss der vehs**tyeh**rer

Het spijt me, alles is uitverkocht.	I'm sorry, we're sold out.
Er zijn alleen nog een paar plaatsen over op het balkon/in de stalles.	There are only a few seats left in the circle (mezzanine)/stalls (orchestra).
Mag ik uw kaartje zien, alstublieft?	May I see your ticket?
Dit is uw plaats.	This is your seat.

Opera—Ballet—Concert

Where's the opera house?	**Waar is het operagebouw?**	ʋaar iss heht **oa**perraa-gherbo^{ow}
Where's the concert hall?	**Waar is het concertgebouw?**	ʋaar iss heht kon**sehrt**-gherbo^{ow}
What's on at the opera tonight?	**Welke opera is er vanavond?**	**ʋehl**ker **oa**perraa iss ehr vahn**aa**vont
Who's singing?	**Wie zingt er?**	ʋee zingt ehr
Who's dancing?	**Wie danst er?**	ʋee dahnst ehr
What time does the programme start?	**Hoe laat begint de voorstelling?**	hoo laat ber**ghint** der **voar**stehling
What orchestra is playing?	**Welk orkest speelt er?**	ʋehlk or**kehst** spaylt ehr
What are they playing?	**Wat spelen ze?**	ʋaht **spay**lern zer
Who's the conductor?	**Wie is de dirigent?**	ʋee iss der deeree**ghehnt**

FOR TIPPING, see page 1

Night-club—Discotheques

Night-clubs and discotheques are the same the world over, so we'll content ourselves with the following:

Can you recommend a good night-club?	**Kunt u mij een goede nachtclub aanbevelen?**	kurnt ew ayn **ghoo**der **nahkht**klurp **aan**bervaylern
Is there a floor show?	**Is er een floorshow?**	iss ehr ayn "floorshow"
What time does the floor show start?	**Hoe laat begint de floorshow?**	hoo laat ber**ghint** der "floorshow"
Is evening dress necessary?	**Is avondkleding noodzakelijk?**	iss **aa**vontklayding noat**zaa**kerlerk

And once inside...

A table for 2, please.	**Een tafel voor 2 personen, alstublieft.**	ayn **taa**ferl voar 2 pehr**soa**nern ahlstew**bleeft**
My name is ... I reserved a table for 4.	**Mijn naam is ... Ik heb een tafel voor 4 personen gereserveerd.**	maiyn naam iss ... ik hehp ayn **taa**ferl voar 4 pehr**soa**nern gherrayzehr**vayrt**
I telephoned you earlier.	**Ik heb u vooraf gebeld.**	ik hehp ew voar**ahf** gher**behlt**
We haven't got a reservation.	**Wij hebben niet gereserveerd.**	ɏaiy **heh**bern neet gheerayzehr**vayrt**

Dancing

Where can we go dancing?	**Waar kunnen we gaan dansen?**	ɏaar **kur**nern ɏer ghaan **dahn**sern
Is there a discotheque in town?	**Is er een discotheek in de stad?**	iss ehr ayn diskoa**tayk** in der staht
Is there an admission charge?	**Moet er toegang betaald worden?**	moot ehr **too**ghahng ber**taalt** **ɏor**dern
There's a dance at the...	**Er is een dansavond in de...**	ehr iss ayn **dahns**aavont in der
Would you like to dance?	**Wilt u dansen?**	ɏilt ew **dahn**sern

RELAXING

Do you happen to play . . . ?

Do you happen to play chess?	**Schaakt u misschien?**	skhaakt ew mers**skheen**
I'm afraid I don't.	**Jammer genoeg niet.**	**yah**merr gher**nookh** neet
No, but I'll give you a game of draughts (checkers).	**Nee, maar ik wil wel met u dammen.**	nay maar ik ʋil ʋehl meht ew **dah**mern

king	**koning**	**koa**ning
queen	**koningin**	**koa**ni**yin**
castle (rook)	**kasteel**	kah**stayl**
bishop	**loper**	**loa**perr
knights	**paard**	paart
pawn	**pion**	pee**yon**
Checkmate!	**Schaakmat!**	**skhaak**maht

Do you play cards?	**Speelt u kaart?**	spaylt ew kaart
bridge	**bridge**	'bridge'
canasta	**canasta**	kaa**nah**staa
poker	**poker**	**poa**kerr
pontoon (21)	**eenentwintigen**	aynehnt**ʋin**terghern
whist	**whist**	ʋist

ace	**aas**	aass
king	**heer**	hayr
queen	**vrouw**	vro^{ow}
jack	**boer**	boor
joker	**joker**	**yoa**kerr
hearts	**harten**	**hahr**tern
diamonds	**ruiten**	**rur**^{ew}tern
clubs	**klaveren**	**klaa**verrern
spades	**schoppen**	**skho**ppern

Casino and gambling

There are two casinos in Holland, in Zandvoort on the coast and in Valkenburg in the south of Holland. Mainly roulette and blackjack are played. They are open all year round from 2 p.m. to 2 a.m. In Belgium there are many casinos.

Entry into a casino requires correct dress and an identity card or passport. You must be over 18 and have a clean record in the gambling world. You need have no doubts about the honesty of the game. Casinos are regularly controlled by government inspectors.

Entrance fees are nominal. A ticket (for a day, a week or a month) will be issued to you for admission. English is usually spoken by the croupiers and dealers of the casinos.

SPELEN INZETTEN! PLACE YOUR BETS!	RIEN NE VA PLUS! NO MORE BETS!

For the more modest gamblers, there is also a national lottery (*Staatsloterij*—staatsloater**raiy**) as well as a *Sport-toto*—**sport**toatoa, where people bet on football teams.

Horse racing is not uncommon in Holland and betting is permitted, although it is usually done at the race-track.

Sports

I'd like to see a/an...	**Ik wil graag een... zien.**	ik ∀il ghraakh ayn ... zeen
boxing match	**bokswedstrijd**	**boks**∀ehtstraiyt
football (soccer) match	**voetbalwedstrijd**	**voot**bahl∀ehststraiyt
ice-hockey match	**ijshockeywedstrijd**	**aiys**hokkee∀ehtstraiyt
Can you get me 2 tickets?	**Kunt u 2 kaartjes voor mij krijgen?**	kurnt ew 2 **kaar**tyerss voar maiy **kraiy**ghern
Who's playing?	**Wie speelt er?**	∀ee **spay**lern ehr

FOR NUMBERS, see page 175

What's the admission charge?	**Wat is de toegangsprijs?**	ꝟaht iss der **too**ghahngspraiyss
Where's the nearest golf course?	**Waar is het dichtstbijzijnde golferrein?**	ꝟaar iss heht dikhtstbaiy**zaiyn**der **gholf**tehraiyn
Where are the tennis courts?	**Waar zijn de tennisbanen?**	ꝟaar zaiyn der **teh**nissbaanern
Can I hire rackets?	**Kan ik raketten huren?**	kahn ik raa**keh**ttern **hew**rern
What's the charge per...?	**Wat kost het per...?**	ꝟaht kost heht pehr
day/hour/round	**dag/uur/spel**	dahkh/ewr/spehl
Do I have to sign up beforehand?	**Moet ik van te voren reserveren?**	moot ik vahn ter **voa**rern rayzehr**vay**rern
Where can I hire a bike?	**Waar kan ik een fiets huren?**	ꝟaar kahn ik ayn feets **hew**rern
Where's the nearest race course (track)?	**Waar is de dichtstbijzijnde renbaan?**	ꝟaar iss der dikhtst-baiy**zaiyn**der **rehn**baan
Is there a bowling alley here?	**Is er hier een kegelbaan in de buurt?**	iss ehr heer ayn **kay**gherl-baan in der bewrt
Is there a swimming pool here?	**Is hier een zwembad in de buurt?**	iss heer ayn **zꝟehm**baht in der bewrt
Is it open-air or indoors?	**Is het in de open lucht of overdekt?**	iss heht in der **oa**pern lurkht of oaverr**dehkt**
Is it heated?	**Is het verwarmd?**	iss heht verr**ꝟahrmt**
Can one swim in the lake/river?	**Kan men in het meer/in de rivier zwemmen?**	kahn mahn in heht mayr/ in der **reeveer** **zꝟeh**mern
Is there any good fishing around here?	**Kun je hier in de buurt goed vissen?**	kurn yer heer in der bewrt ghoot **vi**ssern
Do I need a permit?	**Heb ik hiervoor een vergunning nodig?**	hehp ik **heer**voar ayn verr**ghur**ning **noa**derkh
Where can I get one?	**Waar kan ik die krijgen?**	ꝟaar kahn ik dee **kraiy**ghern

On the beach

With one fifth of its surface covered with lakes, canals and rivers, Holland is an ideal country for all types of water-sports. Boating, fishing, swimming, water-skiing and surfing are possible wherever you go in the lake districts and along the North Sea coast, with its 150 miles of sandy beaches. For information concerning boat hires, fishing restrictions and maps of local waterways, contact the local VVV office.

Is it safe for swimming?	**Kan men hier veilig zwemmen?**	kahn mehn heer **vaiy**lerkh z**veh**mern
Is there a life-guard?	**Is er hier een reddingsbrigade?**	iss ehr heer ayn **reh**dingsbreeghaader
Is it safe for children?	**Is het hier veilig voor kinderen?**	iss heht heer **vaiy**lerkh voar **kin**derrern
The sea is very calm.	**De zee is erg kalm.**	der zay iss ehrkh kahlm
There are some big waves.	**Er zijn grote golven.**	ehr zaiyn **ghroa**ter **ghol**vern
Are there any danger-ous currents?	**Zijn er gevaarlijke stromingen?**	zaiyn ehr gher**vaar**lerker **stroa**mingern
What time is high/ low tide?	**Wanneer is het vloed/eb?**	vah**nayr** iss heht vloot/ ehp
What's the temper-ature of the water?	**Hoeveel graden is het water?**	hoo**vayl ghraa**dern iss heht **vaa**terr
I want to hire a/ an/some...	**Ik wil graag ... huren.**	ik vil ghraakh ... **hew**rern
air mattress	**een luchtbed**	ayn **lurkht**beht
bathing hut	**een badhokje**	ayn **baht**hokyer
deck-chair	**een badstoel**	ayn **baht**stool
sunshade	**een parasol**	ayn paaraa**sol**
surfboard	**een surfplank**	ayn **surrf**plahnk
water-skis	**een paar waterski's**	ayn paar **vaa**terrskeess
Where can I hire a ...?	**Waar kan ik... huren?**	vaar kahn ik ... **hew**rern
canoe	**een kano**	ayn **kaa**noa
motorboat	**een motorboot**	ayn **moa**terrboat
rowing-boat	**een roeiboot**	ayn **roo••**boat
sailing-boat	**een zeilboot**	ayn **zaiyl**boat
What's the charge per hour?	**Wat kost het per uur?**	hoo**vayl** kost heht pehr ewr

Before you take a swim, you will want perhaps to ask your neighbour on the beach:

Could you look after this a moment, please?	**Kunt u hier even op letten, alstublieft?**	kurnt ew heer **ay**vern op lehtern ahlstew**bleeft**

PRIVESTRAND PRIVATE BEACH	VERBODEN TE ZWEMMEN NO BATHING

Other sports

There are many skating rinks in Holland, of which some are indoor. They are generally open from mid-October to March and a few months longer for the indoor rinks.

Is there a skating rink here?	**Is hier een ijsbaan in de buurt?**	iss heer ayn **aiyss**baan in der bewrt
I want to hire some skates.	**Ik wil graag een paar schaatsen huren.**	ik ∀il ghraakh ayn paar **skhaat**sern **hew**rern

Gliding *(zweefvliegen)* has become a popular sport in Holland. Many gliding week-ends are organized by clubs scattered all over the country. The minimum age is 14.

Camping—Countryside

There are many excellent camping sites in Holland and Belgium. No special permit is required. Charges vary from place to place, and it might therefore be better to inquire about the fees immediately upon arrival so as to avoid any misunderstanding when settling the bill. The Netherlands National Tourist Office and local VVV offices will provide you with lists of camping sites. Camping is only permitted on specially designated sites.

Can we camp here?	**Mogen we hier kamperen?**	moaghern ʋer heer kahm**payr**ern
Is there a camping site near here?	**Is hier een kampeer-terrein in de buurt?**	iss ehr heer ayn kahm-**payr**tehraiyn in der bewrt
Have you room for a tent/caravan (trailer)?	**Hebt u plaats voor een tent/caravan?**	hehpt ew plaats voar ayn tehnt/"caravan"
May we camp in your field?	**Mogen we onze tent op uw land neerzetten?**	moaghern ʋer **on**zer tehnt op ew^{ee} lahnt **nayr**zehtern
Can we park our caravan here?	**Mogen we onze caravan hier neer-zetten?**	moaghern ʋer **on**zer "caravan" heer **nayr**zehtern
Is this an official camping site?	**Is dit een officieel kampeerterrein?**	iss dit ayn offee**syayl** kahm**payr**tehraiyn
May we light a fire?	**Mogen we een vuurtje maken?**	moaghern ʋer ayn **vewr**tyer **maa**kern
Is there drinking water?	**Is er drinkwater?**	iss ehr **drink**ʋaaterr
Are there shopping facilities on the site?	**Is er een winkel op het kampeerterrein?**	iss ehr ayn **ʋin**kerl op heht kahm**payr**tehraiyn
Are there...?	**Zijn er...?**	zaiyn ehr
baths	**badgelegenheden**	**baht**gherlayghernhaydern
showers	**douches**	**doo**sherss
toilets	**toiletten**	tʋaa**leh**tern

What's the charge...?	**Wat kost het...?**	vaht kost heht
per day	**per dag**	pehr dahkh
per person	**per persoon**	pehr perr**soan**
per child	**per kind**	pehr kint
for a car	**voor een auto**	voar ayn **o^{ow}**toa
for a tent	**voor een tent**	voar ayn tehnt
for a caravan (trailer)	**voor een caravan**	voar ayn "caravan"
Is the tourist tax included?	**Is de belasting erbij inbegrepen?**	iss der ber**lah**sting ehr**baiy** **in**berghraypern
Is there a youth hostel near here?	**Is hier een jeugdherberg in de buurt?**	iss hier ayn **yurght**-hehrbehrgh in der bewrt
Do you know anyone who can put us up for the night?	**Kent u iemand die ons vannacht kan herbergen?**	kehnt ew **ee**mahnt dee onss vahn**nahkht** kahn **hehr**behrghern

VERBODEN TE KAMPEREN	VERBODEN VOOR CARAVANS
NO CAMPING	NO CARAVANS (TRAILERS)

Landmarks

barn	**de schuur**	der skhewr
bridge	**de brug**	der brurkh
brook	**het beekje**	heht **bay**kyer
building	**het gebouw**	heht gher**bo^{ow}**
canal	**het kanaal**	heht kaa**naal**
chimney	**de schoorsteen**	der **skhoar**stayn
church	**de kerk**	der kehrk
cliff	**de klif**	der klif
copse	**het hakhout**	heht **hahk**ho^{ow}t
cottage	**de hut**	der hurt
crossroads	**het kruispunt**	heht **krur^{ew}**spurnt
dike	**de dijk**	der daiyk
farm	**de boerderij**	der boorder**raiy**
ferry	**de veer**	der vayr
field	**het veld**	heht vehlt
footpath	**het voetpad**	heht **voot**paht
forest	**het bos**	heht boss

hamlet	**het gehucht**	heht gher**hurkht**
heath	**de hei**	der haiy
highway	**de grote weg**	der **ghroa**ter ꝟehkh
hill	**de heuvel**	der **hur**verl
house	**het huis**	heht hur^{ew}ss
inn	**de herberg**	der **hehr**behrkh
lake	**het meer**	heht mayr
lighthouse	**de vuurtoren**	der **vewr**toarern
marsh	**het moeras**	heht moo**rahss**
moorland	**de heide**	der **haiy**der
ocean	**de oceaan**	der oasee**yaan**
path	**het pad**	heht paht
pond	**de vijver**	der **vaiy**verr
pool	**de plas**	der plahss
river	**de rivier**	der ree**veer**
road	**de weg**	der ꝟehkh
road sign	**het verkeersbord**	heht verr**kayrs**bort
sea	**de zee**	der zay
spring	**de bron**	der bron
stream	**de stroom**	der stroam
swamp	**het moeras**	heht moo**rahss**
telegraph pole	**de telefoonpaal**	der tayler**foan**paal
track	**het pad**	heht paht
tree	**de boom**	der boam
village	**het dorp**	heht dorp
waterfall	**de waterval**	der **ꝟaa**terrvahl
well	**de put**	der purt
wood	**het bos**	heht bos
What's the name of that river?	**Hoe heet die rivier?**	hoo hayt dee ree**veer**
Are we below/above sea level?	**Bevinden we ons beneden/boven zeeniveau?**	ber**vin**dern ꝟer onss ber**nay**dern/**boa**vern **zay**neevoa
Is there a scenic route to...?	**Is er een mooie weg naar...?**	iss ehr ayn **moa**^{ee}yer ꝟehkh naar

... and if you're tired of walking, you can always try hitch-hiking (*liften*—**lif**tern).

Can you give me a lift to...?	**Kunt u mij een lift geven naar...?**	kurnt ew maiy ayn lift **ghay**vern naar

FOR ASKING THE WAY, see page 144

Making friends

Introductions

A few phrases to get you started:

May I introduce Miss...?	**Mag ik u juffrouw... even voorstellen?**	mahkh ik ew **yurfro**^{ow} ayvern **voar**stehlern
Glad to know you.	**Aangenaam kennis te maken.**	aangher**naam keh**niss ter maakern
How do you do?	**Hoe maakt u het?**	hoo maakt ew heht
Very well, thank you.	**Uitstekend, dank u.**	ur^{ew}**tstay**kernt dahnk ew
Fine, thanks. And you?	**Best, dank u. En u?**	behst dahnk ew∀. ehn ew
I'd like you to meet a friend of mine.	**Ik zou u graag aan een vriend van mij willen voorstellen.**	ik zo^{ow} ew ghraakh aan ayn vreent vahn maiy **∀**illern **voar**stehlern
John, this is...	**John, dit is...**	john dit iss
My name is...	**Ik heet...**	ik hayt
...sends his/her best regards.	**U krijgt heel veel groeten van...**	ew kraight hayl vayl **ghroo**tern vahn

Follow-up

How long have you been here?	**Hoe lang bent u hier al?**	hoo lahng behnt ew heer ahl
We've been here a week.	**Wij zijn hier al een week.**	∀aiy zaiyn heer ahl ayn ∀ayk
Is this your first visit?	**Bent u hier voor de eerste keer?**	behnt ew heer voar der **ayr**ster kayr
No, we came here last year.	**Nee, we zijn hier verleden jaar ook geweest.**	nay ∀er zaiyn heer veer-laydern yaar oak gher**∀ayst**

Are you enjoying your stay?	**Bevalt het u hier?**	ber**vahlt** heht ew heer
Yes, I like it very much.	**Ja, het bevalt mij heel goed.**	yaa heht ber**vahlt** maiy hayl ghoot
I like the landscape a lot.	**Ik vind dit landschap erg mooi.**	ik vint dit **lahnts**khahp ehrkh moo^{ee}
Are you on your own?	**Bent u alleen?**	behnt ew ah**layn**
I'm with...	**Ik ben hier met...**	ik behn heer meht
my children	**mijn kinderen**	maiyn **kin**derrern
my wife	**mijn vrouw**	maiyn vro^{ow}
my husband	**mijn man**	maiyn mahn
my family	**mijn gezin**	maiyn gher**zin**
my parents	**mijn ouders**	maiyn **o^{ow}**derrss
some friends	**vrienden**	**vreen**dern
Where do you come from?	**Waar komt u vandaan?**	ꝟaar komt ew vahn**daan**
What part of ... do you come from?	**Uit welk gedeelte van ... komt u?**	ur^{ew}t ꝟehlk gher**dayl**ter vahn ... komt ew
I'm from ...	**Ik kom uit...**	ik kom ur^{ew}t
Where are you staying?	**Waar verblijft u?**	ꝟaar verr**blaiyft** ew
We're camping.	**Wij kamperen.**	ꝟaiy kahm**pay**rern
We're here on holiday.	**Wij zijn hier met vakantie.**	ꝟaiy zaiyn heer meht vaa**kahn**see
I'm a student.	**Ik ben student.**	ik behn stew**dehnt**
What are you studying?	**Wat studeert u?**	ꝟaht stew**dayrt** ew
I'm here on a business trip.	**Ik ben hier voor zaken.**	ik behn heer voar **zaa**kern
What kind of business are you in?	**Wat voor zaken doet u?**	ꝟaht voar **zaa**kern doot ew
I hope we'll see you again soon.	**Ik hoop dat we elkaar gauw weerzien.**	ik hoap daht ꝟer ehl**kaar** gho^{ow} **ꝟay**rzeen
See you later!	**Tot ziens!**	tot seenss
See you tomorrow!	**Tot morgen!**	tot **mor**ghern
We'll certainly see each other again one of these days.	**We zullen elkaar zeker weerzien een dezer dagen.**	ꝟer **zur**lern ehl**kaar** **zay**kerr **ꝟay**rzeen ayn **day**zerr **daa**ghern

Weather ... or not

Always a popular subject:

What a lovely day!	**Wat een prachtig weer!**	Ꝟaht ayn **prahkh**terkh Ꝟayr
What awful weather!	**Wat een afschuwelijk weer!**	Ꝟaht ayn ahf**skhew**Ꝟerlerk Ꝟayr
Cold today, isn't it?	**Koud vandaag, vindt u niet?**	ko^{ow}t vahn**daakh** vint ew neet
Isn't it hot today?	**Wat een hitte vandaag, nietwaar?**	Ꝟaht ayn **hit**ter vahn**daakh** neet**Ꝟaar**
Is it usually as warm as this?	**Is het hier altijd zo warm?**	iss heht heer **ahl**taiyt zoa Ꝟahrm
What's the temperature like outside?	**Wat is de temperatuur buiten?**	Ꝟaht iss der tehmperraa**tewr** **bur**^{ew}tern
The wind's up.	**Het waait.**	heht Ꝟaa^{ee}t
What a fog!	**Wat een mist!**	Ꝟaht ayn mist
Do you think it'll ... tomorrow?	**Denkt u dat het morgen...?**	dehnkt ew daht heht **mor**ghern
clear up	**op zal klaren**	op zahl **klaa**rern
rain	**regent**	**ray**ghernt
snow	**sneeuwt**	snay^{oo}t
be sunny	**zonnig weer is**	**zon**nerkh Ꝟayr iss

Invitations

My wife/My husband and I would like you to dine with us on Friday.	**Mijn vrouw/Mijn man en ik willen u graag op vrijdag voor een etentje uitnodigen.**	maiyn vro^{ow}/maiyn mahn ehn ik **Ꝟi**llern ew ghraakh op **vraiy**dahkh voar ayn **ay**terntyer **ur**^{ew}**t**noaderghern
Can you come to dinner tomorrow night?	**Kunt u morgenavond bij ons komen eten?**	kurnt ew **mor**ghern-aavont baiy onss **koa**mern **ay**tern
Can you come over for cocktails this evening?	**Komt u vanavond een borreltje drinken?**	komt ew vahn**aa**vont ayn **bor**rerltyer **drin**kern
There's a party. Are you coming?	**Er wordt een feestje gehouden. Komt u ook?**	ehr Ꝟort ayn **fays**tyer gher**ho**^{ow}dern. komt ew ook

That's very kind of you.	**Dat is bijzonder vriendelijk van u.**	daht iss bee**zon**derr **vreen**derlenk vahn ew
Great! I'd love to come.	**Ik kom dolgraag!**	ik kom **dol**ghraakh
What time shall we come?	**Hoe laat verwacht u ons?**	hoo laat verr**ʋahkht** ew onss
May I bring a friend/ girl friend?	**Mag ik een vriend/ vriendin meenemen?**	mahkh ik ayn vreent/ vreen**din may**naymern
I'm afraid we've got to go.	**Helaas moeten we nu weg.**	hay**laass moo**tern ʋer new ʋehkh
Next time you must come to visit us.	**De volgende keer moet u bij ons komen.**	der **vol**ghernder kayr moot ew baiy onss **koa**mern
Thanks for the evening. It was great.	**Hartelijk bedankt voor de gezellige avond. Het was fantastisch.**	**hahr**terlerk ber**dahnkt** voar der gher**zeh**lergher **aa**vont. heht ʋahss fahn**tahs**teess

Dating

Can I get you a drink?	**Wilt u iets drinken?**	ʋilt ew eets **drin**kern
Would you like a cigarette?	**Wilt u een sigaret?**	ʋilt ew ayn seeghaa**reht**
Do you have a light, please?	**Hebt u een vuurtje, alstublieft?**	hehpt ew ayn **vewr**tyer ahlstew**bleeft**
Excuse me, could you please help me?	**Neemt u mij niet kwalijk, kunt u mij misschien helpen?**	naymt ew maiy neet **kʋaa**lerk kurnt ew maiy mers**skheen hehl**pern
I'm lost. Can you show me the way to...?	**Ik ben de weg kwijt. Kunt u mij de weg naar ... wijzen?**	ik behn der ʋehkh kʋaiyt. kurnt ew maiy der ʋehkh naar ... **ʋaiy**zern
Are you waiting for someone?	**Wacht u op iemand?**	ʋahkht ew op **ee**mahnt
Leave me alone, please!	**Laat me met rust, alstublieft!**	laat mer meht rurst ahlstew**bleeft**
Are you free this evening?	**Bent u vanavond vrij?**	behnt ew vahn**aa**vont vraiy
Thank you, I've got another engagement this evening.	**Nee, dank u. Ik heb al een andere afspraak voor vanavond.**	nay dahnk ew. ik hehp ahl ayn **ahn**derrer **ahf**spraak voar vahn**aa**vont

Would you like to go out with me tomorrow evening?	**Hebt u zin om morgenavond met mij uit te gaan?**	hehpt ew zin om **mor**ghernaavont meht maiy ur^{ew}t ter ghaan
Would you like to go dancing?	**Hebt u zin om te gaan dansen?**	hehpt ew zin om ter ghaan **dahn**sern
I know a good discotheque.	**Ik weet een goede discotheek.**	ik Ꝟayt ayn **ghoo**der diskoa**tayk**
Shall we go to the cinema (movies)?	**Zullen we naar de bioscoop gaan?**	**zur**lern Ꝟer naar der beeyos**koap** ghaan
Where shall we meet?	**Waar zullen we afspreken?**	Ꝟaar **zur**lern Ꝟer **ahf**spraykern
I'll pick you up at your hotel.	**Ik kom u in uw hotel afhalen.**	ik kom ew in ew^{oo} hoa**tehl** **ahf**haalern
I'll call for you at 8.	**Ik kom u om 8 uur afhalen.**	ik kom ew om 8 ewr **ahf**haalern
Would you like to go for a drive?	**Hebt u zin om een eindje te gaan rijden?**	hehpt ew zin om ayn **aiyn**tyer ter ghaan **raiy**dern
No, I'm not interested, thank you.	**Nee, ik voel er niet voor, dank u.**	nay ik vool ehr neet voar dahnk ew
May I take you home?	**Mag ik u naar huis brengen?**	mahkh ik ew naar hur^{ew}ss **brehng**ern
Can I see you again tomorrow?	**Zie ik u morgen weer?**	zee ik ew **mor**ghern Ꝟayr
Thank you, I've enjoyed myself tremendously.	**Dank u wel, ik heb geweldig genoten.**	dahnk ew Ꝟehl ik hehp gher**Ꝟehl**derkh gher**noa**tern
What's your telephone number?	**Wat is uw telefoonnummer?**	Ꝟaht iss ew^{oo} tayler**foan**nurmerr
Do you live alone?	**Woont u alleen?**	Ꝟoant ew ah**layn**
What time is your last bus/train?	**Hoe laat gaat uw laatste bus/trein?**	hoo laat ghaat ew^{oo} **laat**ster burss/traiyn

Shopping guide

This shopping guide is designed to help you find what you want with ease, accuracy and speed. It features:

1. a list of all major shops, stores and services (p. 98)
2. some general expressions required when shopping to allow you to be specific and selective (p. 100)
3. full details of the shops and services most likely to concern you. Here you'll find advice, alphabetical lists of items and conversion charts listed under the headings below.

Shops—Stores—Services

Shops are usually open Monday to Friday from 8.30/9 a.m. to 5.30/6 p.m. and on Saturdays till 4 p.m. (food shops). Most businesses except department stores close during lunch-time. In many towns, shopkeepers have introduced late closing on either Thursday or Friday night. Department stores and many other shops are closed on Monday morning. Food shops, however, close one afternoon a week. In holiday centres and seaside resorts, you'll find shops open in the evening and during the weekend.

Where's the nearest...?	**Waar is de/het dichtstbijzijnde...?**	√aar iss der/heht dikhtstbaiy**zaiy**nder
antique shop	**de antiekwinkel**	der ahn**teek**√inkerl
baker	**de bakker**	der **bah**kerr
barber	**de herenkapper**	der **hay**rernkahperr
beauty salon	**de schoonheidssalon**	der **skhoan**haiytssaalon
bookshop	**de boekhandel**	der **book**hahnderl
butcher	**de slagerij**	der slaagher**raiy**
chemist's	**de apotheek**	der ahpoa**tayk**
confectioner	**de banketbakkerij**	der bahnkehtbahker**raiy**
dairy	**de melkwinkel, zuivelhandel**	der **mehlk**√inkerl **zur^{ew}**verlhahnderl
delicatessen	**de delicatessenzaak**	der dayleekaa**teh**ssernzaak
department store	**het warenhuis**	heht **√aa**rernhur^{ew}ss
drugstore	**de drogisterij**	der droaghister**raiy**
dry-cleaner	**de stomerij**	der stoamer**raiy**
fishmonger	**de vishandel**	der **viss**hahnderl
flea market	**de vlooienmarkt**	der **vloa**yernmahrkt
florist	**de bloemist**	der bloo**mist**
furrier	**de bontzaak**	der **bont**zaak
greengrocer	**de groenteboer**	der **ghroon**terboor
grocery	**de kruideniers-winkel**	der krur^{ew}der**neers**√inkerl
hairdresser (ladies')	**de dameskapper**	der **daa**merskahperr
hairdresser (men's)	**de herenkapper**	der **hay**rernkahperr
hardware store	**de ijzerhandel**	der **aiy**zerrhahnderl
health-food store	**de reformawinkel**	der rer**for**maa√inkerl
jeweller	**de juwelier**	der yew√er**leer**
launderette	**de wasserette**	der √ahsser**reh**ter
laundry	**de wasserij**	der √ahsser**raiy**
liquor store	**de slijterij**	der slaiyter**raiy**

market	**de markt**	der mahrkt
milliner	**de hoedenwinkel**	der hoodernʋinkerl
newsagent	**de krantenverkoper**	der krahnternverrkoaperr
news-stand	**de krantenkiosk**	der krahnternkeeyosk
off-licence	**de slijterij**	der slaiyterraiy
optician	**de opticiën**	der opteessyehn
pharmacy	**de apotheek**	der ahpoatayk
photo shop	**de fotozaak**	der foatoazaak
shoemaker (repairs)	**de schoenmaker**	der skhoonmaakerr
shoe shop	**de schoenwinkel**	der skhoonʋinkerl
souvenir shop	**de souvenirwinkel**	der sooverneerʋinkerl
sporting goods shop	**de sportzaak**	der sportzaak
stationer	**de kantoorboek-handel**	der kahntoarbookhahnderl
supermarket	**de supermarkt**	der sewperrmahrkt
tailor	**de kleermaker**	der klayrmaakerr
tobacconist	**de sigarenwinkel**	der seeghaarernʋinkerl
toy shop	**de speelgoedwinkel**	der spaylghootʋinkerl
watchmaker	**de horlogemaker**	der horloazhermaakerr
wine merchant	**de wijnhandel**	der ʋaiynhahnderl

…and some further useful addresses:

bank	**de bank**	der bahnk
currency-exchange office	**het wisselkantoor**	heht ʋisserlkahntoar
dentist	**de tandarts**	der tahntahrts
doctor	**de dokter**	der dokterr
hospital	**het ziekenhuis**	heht zeekernhur^ew^ss
lost-property (lost and found) office	**het bureau voor gevonden voor-werpen**	heht bewroa voar ghervondern voarʋehr-pern
police station	**het politiebureau**	heht poaleetseebewroa
post office	**het postkantoor**	heht postkahntoar
tourist office	**het VVV-kantoor**	heht vayvayvay-kahntoar
travel agent	**het reisbureau**	heht raiysbewroa

UITVERKOOP	**SALE**

General expressions

Where?

Where's a good ...?	**Waar is een goede ...?**	ʋaar iss ayn **ghooder**
Where's the nearest ...?	**Waar is de dichtstbijzijnde ...?**	ʋaar iss der dikhtst-baiyzaiynder
Where can I find a ...?	**Waar kan ik een ... vinden?**	ʋaar kahn is ayn ... vindern
Can you recommend a cheap ...?	**Kunt u een goedkope ... aanbevelen?**	kurnt ew ayn ghoot**koaper** ... aanbervaylern
Where's the main shopping centre?	**Waar is het winkelcentrum?**	ʋaar iss heht **ʋinkerl**-sehntrurm
How far is it from here?	**Hoe ver is het hier vandaan?**	hoo vehr iss heht heer vandaan
Where's the cashier's?	**Waar is de kassa?**	ʋaar iss der **kahsaa**

Service

Can you help me?	**Kunt u mij helpen?**	kurnt ew maiy **hehlpern**
I'm just looking around.	**Ik kijk alleen even rond.**	ik kaiyk ah**layn** ayvern ront
I want ...	**Ik wil ... hebben.**	ik ʋil ... **hehbern**
Can you show me some ...?	**Kunt u mij ... laten zien?**	kurnt ew maiy ... **laatern** zeen
Do you have any ...?	**Hebt u ...?**	hehpt ew

That one

Can you show me ...?	**Kunt u mij ... laten zien?**	kurnt ew maiy ... **laatern** zeen
this/that	**dit/dat**	dit/daht
the one in the window/in the display case	**die in de etalage/ in de uitstalkast**	dee in der aytaa**laa**zher/ in der **ur^{ew}t**stahlkahst
It's over there.	**Daar is het.**	daar iss heht

Defining the article

I'd like a ... one.	**Ik wil graag een ... hebben**	ik ∀il ghraakh ayn ... **heh**bern

big	**grote**	**ghroa**ter
cheap	**goedkope**	ghoot**koa**per
coloured	**gekleurde**	gher**klurr**der
dark	**donkere**	**don**kerrer
large	**grote**	**ghroa**ter
light (weight)	**lichte**	**likh**ter
light (colour)	**lichte**	**likh**ter
round	**ronde**	**ron**der
small	**kleine**	**klaiy**ner
soft	**zachte**	**zahkh**ter
square	**vierkante**	**veer**kahnter

Preference

Haven't you anything...?	**Hebt u niet iets...?**	hehpt ew neet eets
cheaper/better	**goedkopers/beters**	ghoot**koa**perrss/**bay**terrss
larger/smaller	**groters/kleiners**	**ghroa**terrss/**klaiy**nerrss
Can you show me some more?	**Kunt u mij nog wat laten zien?**	kurnt ew maiy nokh ∀aht **laa**tern zeen

How much?

How much is it?	**Hoeveel kost dit?**	hoo**vayl** kost dit
How much are they?	**Hoeveel kosten ze?**	hoo**vayl kos**tern zer
Please write it down.	**Schrijft u het alstublieft even op.**	skhraiyft ew heht ahls-tew**bleeft ay**vern op
I don't want to spend more than ... guilders.	**Ik wil niet meer dan ...gulden uitgeven.**	ik ∀il neet mayr dahn ...**ghurl**dern ur^{ew}tghayvern

Decision

That's just what I want.	**Dat is precies wat ik zoek.**	daht iss prer**seess** ∀aht ik zook
It's not (quite) what I want.	**Dat is niet (precies) wat ik zoek.**	daht iss neet (prer**seess**) ∀aht ik zook

FOR COLOURS, see page 113

No, I don't like it.	**Nee, het bevalt mij niet.**	nay heht ber**vahlt** maiy neet
I'll take this one.	**Ik neem dit.**	ik naym dit

Ordering

Can you order it for me?	**Kunt u het voor mij bestellen?**	kurnt ew heht voar maiy ber**steh**lern
How long will it take?	**Hoe lang duurt het?**	hoo lahng dewrt heht
I'd like it as soon as possible.	**Ik zou het zo gauw mogelijk willen hebben.**	ik zo^{ow} heht zoa go^{ow} **moa**gherlerk **ʋi**llern **heh**bern

Delivery

I'll take it with me.	**Ik neem het mee.**	ik naym heht may
Deliver it to the ... Hotel.	**Stuurt u het naar het ... Hotel.**	stewrt ew heht naar heht ... hoa**tehl**
Please send it to this address.	**Stuurt u het alstublieft naar dit adres.**	stewrt ew heht ahlstew**bleeft** naar dit aa**drehss**
Will I have any difficulty with the customs?	**Krijg ik geen moeilijkheden met de douane?**	kraiykh ik ghayn **moo**^{ee}lerkhaydern meht der doo**ʋaa**ner

Paying

How much is it?	**Hoeveel is het?**	**hoo**vayl kost heht
Can I pay by traveller's cheque?	**Kan ik met reischeques betalen?**	kahn ik meht **raiys**shehks ber**taa**lern
Do you accept credit cards?	**Neemt u kredietkaarten aan?**	naymt ew krer**deet**kaartern aan
Haven't you made a mistake in the bill?	**Hebt u geen vergissing in de rekening gemaakt?**	hehpt ew ghayn verr**ghi**ssing in der **ray**kerning gher**maakt**
Could I have a receipt, please?	**Mag ik een kwitantie van u hebben, alstublieft?**	mahkh ik ayn kʋee**tahnt**see vahn ew **heh**bern ahlstew**bleeft**
Could I have a plastic bag, please?	**Mag ik een plastic zak van u hebben, alstublieft?**	mahkh ik ayn **pleh**steek zahk vahn ew **heh**bern ahlstew**bleeft**

FOR NUMBERS, see page 175

Anything else?

No, thanks, that's all.	**Nee, dank u, dat is alles.**	nay dahnk ew daht iss ahlerss
Yes, I want...	**Ja, ik wil graag...**	yaa ik ʋil ghraakh
Show me...	**Laat u ... even zien.**	laat ew ... ayvern zeen
Thank you.	**Dank u wel.**	dahnk ew ʋehl
Good-bye.	**Tot ziens.**	tot seenss

Dissatisfied

Can you please exchange this?	**Kan ik dit ruilen, alstublieft?**	kahn ik dit rur[ew]lern ahlstewbleeft
I want to return this.	**Ik wil dit teruggeven.**	ik ʋil dit terrurghghayvern
I'd like a refund.	**Ik wil graag mijn geld terug.**	ik ʋil ghraakh maiyn ghehlt terrurkh
Here's the receipt.	**Hier is de kwitantie.**	heer iss der kʋeetahnsee

Kan ik u helpen?	Can I help you?
Welke ... wilt u hebben?	What ... would you like?
kleur/model	colour/shape
kwaliteit/hoeveelheid	quality/quantity
Het spijt mij, maar dat hebben we niet.	I'm sorry, we haven't any.
Zullen wij het voor u bestellen?	Shall we order it for you?
Wilt u het meenemen of zullen wij het u toesturen?	Will you take it with you or shall we send it?
Nog iets?	Anything else?
Dat is dan ... gulden, alstublieft.	That's ... guilders, please.
De kassa is daar.	The cashier's over there.
Wij nemen geen krediet-kaarten/reischeques aan.	We don't accept credit cards/ traveller's cheques.

Bookshop—Stationer's—News-stand

In Holland, bookshops and stationers' are usually separate shops, although the latter will often sell paperbacks. Newspapers and magazines in English and other languages are sold in kiosks and in many bookshops as well as in hotels.

Where's the nearest...?	**Waar is de dichtst-bijzijnde...?**	vaar iss der dikhtst-baiyzaiynder
bookshop	**boekhandel**	bookhahnderl
news-stand	**krantenkiosk**	krahnternkeeyosk
stationer	**kantoorboekhandel**	kahntoarbookhahnderl
Where can I buy a newspaper in English?	**Waar kan ik een Engelse krant kopen?**	vaar kahn ik ayn ehngerlsser krahnt koapern
I want to buy a/an/some...	**Ik wil graag ... hebben.**	ik vil ghraakh ... hehbern
address book	**een adresboekje**	ayn aadrehsbookyer
ball-point pen	**een ballpoint**	ayn "ballpoint"
blotting paper	**vloeipapier**	vlooeepaapeer
book	**een boek**	ayn book
box of paints	**een verfdoos**	ayn vehrfdoass
carbon paper	**karbonpapier**	kahrbonpaapeer
cellophane tape	**plakband**	plahkbahnt
detective story	**een detectiveverhaal**	ayn daytehkteeververrhaal
dictionary	**een woordenboek**	ayn voardernbook
English-Dutch	**Engels-Nederlands**	ehngerlss/nayderrlahnts
Dutch-English	**Nederlands-Engels**	nayderrlahnts/ehngerlss
drawing pins	**punaises**	pewnehserss
envelopes	**enveloppen**	ehnverloppern
eraser	**een gummetje**	ayn ghurmertyer
exercise book	**een schrift**	ayn skhrift
fountain pen	**een vulpen**	ayn vurlpehn
glue	**lijm**	laiym
guide book	**een reisgids**	ayn raiysghits
ink	**inkt**	inkt
labels	**etiketten**	ayteekehtern
magazine	**een tijdschrift**	ayn taiytskhrift
map	**een landkaart**	ayn lahntkaart
newspaper	**een krant**	ayn krahnt
American/English	**Amerikaanse/Engelse**	aamayreekaansser/ehngerlsser
notebook	**een notitieboekje**	ayn noateetseebookyer
paperback	**een pocketboek**	ayn pokkertbook

paper napkins	**papieren servetten**	paa**peer**ern sehr**veh**tern
paste	**plaksel**	**plahk**serl
pen	**een pen**	ayn **pehn**
pencil	**een potlood**	ayn **pot**loat
pencil sharpener	**een puntenslijper**	ayn **purn**ternslaiyperr
picture book	**een prentenboek**	ayn **prehn**ternbook
playing cards	**een kaartspel**	ayn **kaart**spehl
postcards	**briefkaarten**	**breef**kaartern
refill (for a pen)	**een vulling (voor een pen)**	ayn **vur**ling (voar ayn pehn)
road map	**een wegenkaart**	ayn **√ay**ghernkaart
rubber	**een gummetje**	ayn **ghur**mertyer
rubber bands	**elastiekjes**	aylah**steek**yerss
ruler	**een liniaal**	ayn leenee**yaal**
stamps	**postzegels**	**post**zaygherlss
string	**touw**	too[ow]
thriller	**een detective-verhaal**	ayn daytehk**tee**ver-haal
thumbtacks	**punaises**	pewn**eh**serss
tissue paper	**zijdepapier**	**zaiy**derpaapeer
town map	**een plattegrond**	ayn **plah**terghrond
typewriter ribbon	**een schrijfmachine-lint**	ayn **skhraiyf**maasheener-lint
typing paper	**schrijfmachine-papier**	**skhraiyf**maasheener-paapeer
wrapping paper	**pakpapier**	**pahk**paapeer
writing pad	**een bloknoot**	ayn **blok**noat
Where's the guide book section?	**Waar is de afdeling reisgidsen?**	√aar iss der **ahf**dayling **raiys**ghitsern
Where do you keep the English books?	**Waar staan de Engelse boeken?**	√aar staan der **ehng**erlsser **book**ern
Have you any of ...'s books in English?	**Hebt u een boek van ... in het Engels?**	hehpt ew ayn book vahn... in heht **ehng**erlss

Here are some contemporary Dutch authors whose books are available in English translation:

Simon Carmiggelt
Jan Cremer
Johan Fabricius
Hella Haasse
Jan de Hartog*
Willem Frederik Hermans
Anton Koolhaas
Jan Mens
Harry Mullisch
Maarten Toonder
Adriaan van der Veen
Jan Wolkers

* Jan de Hartog writes in both Dutch and English.

Camping

Here we're concerned with the equipment you may need.

I'd like a/an/ some…	**Ik wil graag … hebben.**	ik ꝟil ghraakh hehbern
aluminium foil	**aluminiumfolie**	ahlew**meeneeyurm**foalee
axe	**een bijl**	ayn baiyl
bottle opener	**een flesopener**	ayn **flehss**oapernerr
bucket	**een emmer**	ayn **eh**merr
butane gas	**butagas**	**bew**taaghahss
camp bed	**een veldbed**	ayn **vehlt**beht
camping equipment	**een kampeer-uitrusting**	ayn kahm**payr**-ur^{ew}trursting
can opener	**een blikopener**	ayn **blik**oapernerr
candles	**wat kaarsen**	ꝟaht **kaar**sern
chair	**een stoel**	ayn stool
charcoal	**houtskool**	**ho^{ow}t**skoal
clothes-pegs	**knijpers**	**knaiy**perrss
compass	**een kompas**	ayn kom**pahss**
corkscrew	**een kurketrekker**	ayn **kurr**kertrehkerr
crockery	**eetgerei**	**ayt**gherraiy
cutlery	**bestek**	ber**stehk**
deck-chair	**een ligstoel**	ayn **dehk**stool
fishing tackle	**visgerei**	**vis**gherraiy
folding chair	**een vouwstoel**	ayn **vo^{ow}**stool
folding table	**een vouwtafel**	ayn **vo^{ow}**taaferl
frying pan	**een koekepan**	ayn **koo**kerpahn
grill	**een braadrooster**	ayn **braat**roasterr
grill spits	**braadspitten**	**braat**spitern
groundsheet	**een grondzeil**	ayn **ghront**zaiyl
hammer	**een hamer**	ayn **haa**merr
hammock	**een hangmat**	ayn **hahng**mahr
haversack	**een proviandtas**	ayn proavee**yahnt**tahss
ice-bag	**een ijszak**	ayn **aiys**zahk
kerosene	**petroleum**	pay**troa**leeyurm
kettle	**een ketel**	ayn **kay**terl
knapsack	**een ransel**	ayn **rahn**tserl
lamp	**een lamp**	ayn lahmp
lantern	**een lantaarn**	ayn **lahn**taarn
matches	**lucifers**	**lew**sseefehrs
mattress	**een matras**	ayn maa**trahss**
methylated spirits	**brandspiritus**	**brahnt**speereeturss
mosquito repellent	**muggenolie**	**murg**hernoalee
nails	**spijkers**	**spaiy**kerrss
pail	**een emmer**	ayn **eh**mmerr
paraffin	**petroleum**	pay**troa**leeyurm

penknife	**een zakmes**	ayn **zahk**mehss
picnic case	**een picknickmand**	ayn **pik**nikmahnt
plastic bags	**plastic zakjes**	**pleh**steek **zahk**yerss
pot	**een pot**	ayn pot
primus stove	**een primus**	ayn **pree**murss
rope	**een touw**	ayn too^{ow}w
rucksack	**een rugzak**	ayn **rurgh**zahk
saucepan	**een pan**	ayn pahn
scissors	**een schaar**	ayn skhaar
screwdriver	**een schroevedraaier**	ayn **skhroo**verdraayerr
sheath knife	**een dolkmes**	ayn **dolk**mehss
sleeping bag	**een slaapzak**	ayn **slaap**zahk
stewpan	**een braadpan**	ayn **braat**pahn
string	**een touw**	ayn to^{ow}
table	**een tafel**	ayn **taa**ferl
tent	**een tent**	ayn tehnt
tent peg	**een haring**	ayn **haa**ring
tent pole	**een tentstok**	ayn **tehnt**stok
thermos flask (bottle)	**een thermosfles**	ayn **tehr**mosflehss
tin opener	**een blikopener**	ayn **blik**oapernerr
tongs	**een nijptang**	ayn **naiyp**tahng
torch	**een zaklantaarn**	ayn **zahk**lahntaarn
water carrier	**een waterzak**	ayn **ʋaa**terrzahk
wood alcohol	**brandspiritus**	**brahnt**speereeturss

Crockery

beakers	**bekers**	**bay**kerrss
cups	**kopjes**	**kop**yerss
mugs	**kroezen**	**kroo**zern
plates	**borden**	**bor**dern
saucers	**schoteltjes**	**skhoa**terltyerss
tumblers	**bekerglazen**	**bay**kerrghlaazern

Cutlery

forks	**vorken**	**vor**kern
knives	**messen**	**meh**ssern
spoons	**lepels**	**lay**perlss
teaspoons	**theelepeltjes**	**tay**layperltyerss
(made of) plastic	**(van) plastic**	(vahn) pleh**steek**
(made of) stainless steel	**(van) roestvrij staal**	(vahn) **roost**vraiy staal

Chemist's—Drugstore

Chemists in Holland usually carry most of the goods you'll find in Britain or the U.S.A. The sign denoting a pharmacy is *Apotheek* (ahpoa**tayk**). In the window of an *apotheek*, you'll see a notice telling you where the nearest all-night chemist's is located.

For perfume, cosmetics and toilet articles you'll have to go to a *drogisterij* (droaghister**raiy**)—drugstore, or non-dispensing chemist's.

This section is divided into two parts:

1. Medicine, first-aid, etc.
2. Toilet articles, cosmetics, etc.

General

Where's the nearest (all-night) chemist's?	**Waar is de dichtst-bijzijnde (dienst-doende) apotheek?**	vaar iss der dikhtst-baiy**zaiy**nder (**deenst**-doonder) ahpoa**tayk**
What time does the chemist's open/close?	**Hoe laat gaat de apotheek open/dicht?**	hoo laat ghaat der ahpoa**tayk oa**pern/dikht

1. Medicines—First-aid

I want something for...	**Ik wil iets tegen ... hebben.**	ik vil eets **tay**ghern ... **heh**bern
a cold	**verkoudheid**	ver**ko**ᵒʷthaiyt
a cough	**hoesten**	**hoos**tern
hay fever	**hooikoorts**	**hoa**ᵉᵉkoarts
a hangover	**een kater**	ayn **kaa**terr
insect bites	**insektenbeten**	in**sehk**ternbaytern
sunburn	**zonnebrand**	**zon**nerbrahnt
travel sickness	**wagenziekte**	**vaa**ghernzeekter
an upset stomach	**indigestie**	indee**ghehs**tee
Can I get it without a prescription?	**Kan ik het zonder recept krijgen?**	kahn ik heht **zon**derr rer**sehpt kraiy**ghern
Do I have to wait?	**Moet ik erop wachten?**	moot ik ehrop **vahkh**tern
When should I come back?	**Wanneer zal ik terugkomen?**	vahn**nayr** zahl ik terr**urgh**-koamern

FOR DOCTOR, see page 162

Can I have a/an some...?	**Mag ik ... van u hebben?**	mahkh ik ... vahn ew **heh**bern
antiseptic cream	**antiseptische crème**	ahntee**sehp**teesser krehm
aspirin	**aspirine**	ahspee**ree**ner
bandage	**verband**	verr**bahnt**
calcium tablets	**calciumtabletten**	**kahl**seeyurmtaablehtern
clinical thermometer	**een koorts-thermometer**	ayn **koarts**tehrmoamayterr
contraceptives	**voorbehoedmiddelen**	**voar**berhootsmidderlern
corn plasters	**likdoornpleisters**	**lik**doarnplaiysterrss
cotton wool	**watten**	**√ah**tern
cough syrup	**een hoestdrank**	ayn **hoost**drahnk
crêpe bandage	**een zwachtel-verband**	ayn **z√ahkh**terlverrbahnt
diabetic lozenges	**tabletten voor diabetici**	taa**bleh**tern voar deeyaa**bay**teessee
disinfectant	**een ontsmettings-middel**	ayn ont**smeh**tingsmidderl
ear drops	**oordruppels**	**oar**drurperlss
eye drops	**oogdruppels**	**oagh**drurperlss
first-aid kit	**een eerste-hulp trommel**	ayn ayrster-**hurlp** tromerl
gargle	**gorgeldrank**	**ghor**gherldrahnk
gauze bandage	**een gaasverband**	ayn **ghaass**verrbahnt
insect repellent	**een insektenwerend middel**	ayn in**sehk**tern√ayrernt midderl
iodine	**jodium**	**yoa**deeyurm
laxative	**laxeermiddel**	lahk**sayr**midderl
lint	**pluksel**	**plurk**serl
nose drops	**neusdruppels**	**nurs**drurperlss
plasters	**pleisters**	**plaiy**sterrss
sanitary napkins	**maandverband**	**maant**verrbahnt
sedative	**pijnstillend middel**	**paiyn**stillernt midderl
sleeping pills	**slaappillen**	**slaap**pillern
tampons	**tampons**	tahm**ponss**
throat lozenges	**tabletten voor de keel**	taa**bleh**tern voar der kayl
tranquillizers	**kalmerende middelen**	kahl**may**rernder midderlern

VERGIF	**POISON**
ALLEEN VOOR UITWENDIG GEBRUIK	**FOR EXTERNAL USE ONLY**

2. Toilet articles—Cosmetics

I'd like a/an/ some...	**Ik zou graag .... willen hebben.**	ik zo^{ow} ghraakh ... **ʋillern hehbern**
acne cream	**een acne zalf**	ayn **ahk**nay zahlf
after shave lotion	**een after shave lotion**	ayn "after-shave" **loa**shern
astringent	**een lotion met samentrekkende werking**	ayn **loa**shern meht **saa**mern-trehkernder **ʋehr**king
bath salts	**badzout**	**baht**zo^{ow}t
Cologne	**een eau de cologne**	ayn oa der kol**loñ**
cream	**een crème**	ayn krehm
for dry/normal/ greasy skin	**voor een droge/ normale/vette huid**	voar ayn **droa**gher nor**maa**ler/**veh**ter hur^{ew}t
cleansing cream	**een cleansing crème**	ayn **klee**nsing krehm
foundation cream	**een basiscrème**	ayn **baa**serskrehm
foot cream	**een voetcrème**	ayn **voot**krehm
hand cream	**een handcrème**	ayn **hahnt**krehm
moisturizing cream	**een vochthou-dende crème**	ayn **vokh**tho^{ow}dernder krehm
night cream	**een nachtcrème**	ayn **nahkht**krehm
cuticle cream	**een nagelriem crème**	ayn **naa**gherlreem krehm
deodorant	**een deodorans**	ayn dayoadoa**rahnss**
emery board	**een kartonnen nagelvijl**	ayn kahr**ton**nern **naa**gherlvaiyl
eye pencil	**een wenkbrauwpot-lood**	ayn **ʋehnk**bro^{ow}potloat
eye shadow	**een oogschaduw**	ayn **oagh**skhaadew^{oo}
face pack	**een gezichtsmasker**	ayn gher**zikhts**mahskerr
face powder	**poeder**	**poo**derr
lipstick	**een lippenstift**	ayn **lip**pernstift
make-up bag	**een make-up tasje**	ayn may**kurp tah**sher
make-up remover pads	**make-up remover pads**	may**kurp** ree**moo**verr pehds
nail brush	**een nagelborsteltje**	ayn **naa**gherlborsterltyer
nail clippers	**een nagelschaartje**	ayn **naa**gherlskhaartyer
nail file	**een nagelvijl**	ayn **naa**gherlvaiyl
nail polish	**nagellak**	**naa**gherllahk
nail polish remover	**een nagellak remover**	ayn **naa**gherllahk ree**moo**verr
nail scissors	**een nagelschaartje**	ayn **naa**gherlskhaartyer
paper handkerchiefs	**papieren zakdoekjes**	paa**pee**rern **zahk**dookyerss
perfume	**parfum**	pahr**furm**

powder	**poeder**	**poo**derr
powder puff	**een poederdons**	ayn **poo**derrdonss
razor	**een scheermes**	ayn **skhayr**mehss
razorblades	**scheermesjes**	**skhayr**mehsherss
rouge	**een rouge**	ayn **roo**zher
cream/powder	**crème/poeder**	krehm/**poo**derr
shaving brush	**een scheerkwast**	ayn **skhayrk**ʋahst
shaving cream	**een scheercrème**	ayn **skhayr**krehm
shaving soap	**een scheerzeep**	ayn **skhayr**zayp
soap	**zeep**	zayp
sponge	**een spons**	ayn sponss
sun tan oil/cream	**een zonnebrandolie/-crème**	ayn **zon**nerbrahntoalee/-krehm
talcum powder	**talkpoeder**	**tahlk**pooderr
tissues	**kleenex-tissues**	**klee**nehks-tisshooss
toilet paper	**toiletpapier**	tʋaa**leht**paapeer
toothbrush	**een tandenborstel**	ayn **tahn**derborsterl
toothpaste	**tandpasta**	**tahnt**pahstaa
tweezers	**een pincet**	ayn pin**seht**

For your hair

bobby pins	**haarspelden**	**haar**spehldern
brush	**een borstel**	ayn **bor**sterl
comb	**een kam**	ayn kahm
curlers	**haarrollers**	**haar**rollerrss
dry shampoo	**droogshampoo**	**droagh**shahmpoa
dye	**verf**	vehrf
grips	**schuifjes**	**skhur**^{ew}fyerss
lacquer	**haarlak**	**haar**lahk
setting lotion	**een haarversteviger**	ayn **haar**verrstayvergherr
shampoo	**shampoo**	shah**m**poa
for dry/greasy hair	**voor droog/vet haar**	voar droakh/veht haar
for dandruff	**tegen roos**	**tay**ghern roass

For the baby

babyfood	**babyvoeding**	babyvooding
bib	**een slabbetje**	ayn **slah**bertyer
dummy (comforter)	**een fopspeen**	ayn **fop**spayn
feeding bottle	**een zuigfles**	ayn **zur**^{ew}**gh**flehss
paper nappies (diapers)	**wegwerp-luiers**	**ʋehgh**ʋehrp-**lur**^{ew}yerrss
plastic nappy holders	**plastic broekjes**	**pleh**steek **broo**kyerss
teat	**een speen**	ayn spayn

Clothing

If you want to buy something specific, prepare yourself in advance. Look at the list of clothing on page 117. Get some idea of the colour, material and size you want. They're listed on the next few pages.

General

I'd like ... for a 10-year-old boy.	**Ik wil graag een ... voor een jongen van 10 jaar.**	ik vil ghraakh ayn ... voar ayn **yongern** vahn 10 yaar
It's for a 4-year-old girl.	**Het is voor een meisje van 4 jaar.**	heht iss ayn **maiysher** vahn 4 yaar
I want something like this.	**Ik wil iets dergelijks hebben.**	ik vil eets **dehr**-gherlerks **hehbern**
I like the one in the window.	**Die in de etalage bevalt mij.**	dee in der ayt**aa**laazher ber**vahlt** maiy
How much is that per metre?	**Hoeveel kost het per meter?**	hoo**vayl** kost heht pehr **may**terr

1 centimetre = 0.39 inch		1 inch = 2.54 cm
1 metre = 39.37 inch		1 foot = 30.5 cm
10 metres = 32.81 ft		1 yard = 0.91 m

Colour

I want something in...	**Ik wil iets in het ... hebben.**	ik vil eets in heht ... **heh**bern
I want a darker/lighter shade.	**Ik wil het iets donkerder/lichter hebben.**	ik vil heht eets **don**kerrderr/**likh**terr **heh**bern
I want something to match this.	**Ik wil iets dat hierbij past hebben.**	ik vil eets daht **heer**baiy pahst **hehbern**
I don't like the colour.	**De kleur bevalt mij niet.**	der klurr ber**vahlt** maiy neet
I'd like it to be the same colour as...	**Ik wil het graag in dezelfde kleur hebben als...**	ik vil heht ghraakh in der**zehlf**der klurr **hehbern** ahlss

FOR CONVERSION TABLES, see pages 185–186

black	**zwart**	z∀ahrt
blue	**blauw**	blo^{ow}
navy blue	**marine-blauw**	maareener blo^{ow}
brown	**bruin**	brur^{ew}n
fawn	**lichtbruin**	**likht**brur^{ew}n
cream	**crème**	krehm
green	**groen**	ghroon
emerald	**smaragdgroen**	smaa**rahght**ghroon
olive	**olijfgroen**	oa**laiyf**ghroon
grey	**grijs**	ghraiyss
mauve	**lila**	**lee**laa
orange	**oranje**	oa**rah**ñer
pink	**rose**	rozer
red	**rood**	roat
crimson	**karmozijnrood**	kahrmoa**zaiyn**roat
purple	**paars**	paarss
rust	**roestkleurig**	**roost**klurrerkh
scarlet	**scharlakenrood**	skhahr**laa**kernroat
silver	**zilver**	**zil**verr
turquoise	**turkoois**	turr**koa^{ee}ss**
violet	**violet**	veeyoa**lent**
white	**wit**	∀it
yellow	**geel**	ghayl
golden	**goudkleurig**	**gho^{ow}t**klurrergh
lemon	**citroengeel**	see**troon**ghayl
light	**licht**	likht
dark	**donker**	**don**kerr

zonder motief (zonderr moateef)

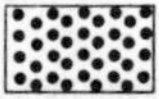

gestippeld (gher**stip**perlt)

gestreept (gher**straypt**)

geruit (gherrur^{ew}t)

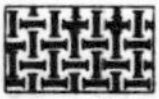

met een motief (meht ayn moateef)

Material

Do you have anything in...?	**Hebt u iets in...?**	hehpt ew eets in
I want something thinner.	**Ik wil iets dunners hebben.**	ik ∀il eets **dur**nerrss **heh**bern
Do you have any better quality?	**Hebt u een betere kwaliteit?**	hehpt ew ayn **bay**terrer k∀aalee**taiyt**

What's it made of?	**Welke stof is het?**	**v̸ehl**ker stof iss heht

cambric	**batist**	baa**tist**
camel-hair	**kameelhaar**	kaa**mayl**haar
corduroy	**ribfluweel**	**rip**flew**v̸ayl**
cotton	**katoen**	kaa**toon**
crêpe	**krip**	krip
denim	**gekeperd katoen**	gher**kay**pert kaa**toon**
felt	**vilt**	vilt
flannel	**flanel**	flaa**nehl**
gabardine	**gabardine**	ghaabahr**deen**er
lace	**kant**	kahnt
leather	**leer**	layr
linen	**linnen**	**lin**nern
nylon	**nylon**	**naiy**lon
pique	**piqué**	pee**kay**
poplin	**popeline**	poaper**leen**er
rubber	**rubber**	**rur**berr
rayon	**kunstzijde**	**kurnst**zaiyder
silk	**zijde**	**zaiy**der
suède	**suède**	se**weh**der
taffeta	**tafzij**	**tahf**zaiyder
terrycloth	**badstof**	**baht**stof
tulle	**tule**	**tew**ler
velvet	**fluweel**	flew**v̸ayl**
velveteen	**katoenfluweel**	kaa**toon**flewv̸ayl
wool	**wol**	v̸ol
worsted	**kamgaren**	**kahm**ghaarern

Can it be...?	**Kan het ... worden?**	kahn heht ... **v̸or**dern
dry-cleaned	**gestoomd**	gher**stoamt**
hand-washed	**met de hand gewassen**	meht der hahnt gher**v̸ah**ssern
machine-washed	**in de machine gewassen**	in der maa**sheen**er gher**v̸ah**ssern
Is it...?	**is het...?**	iss heht
colourfast	**kleurecht**	**klur**rehkht
pure cotton	**100%-katoen**	**hon**derrt proa**sehnt** kaa**toon**
shrink resistant	**krimpvrij**	**krimp**vraiy
synthetic	**synthetisch**	sin**tay**teess
wash and wear	**no-iron**	"no-iron"
wrinkle resistant	**kreukvrij**	**krurk**vraiy

Size

In Europe sizes vary somewhat from country to country, so the following must be taken as an approximate guide.

Ladies

Dresses/Suits							
American	8	10	12	14	16	18	20
British	30	32	34	36	38	40	42
Continental	36	38	40	42	44	46	48

Stockings						
American/British	8	8½	9	9½	10	10½
Continental	0	1	2	3	4	5

Shoes				
American	6	7	8	9
British	4½	5½	6½	7½
Continental	37	38	40	41

Gentlemen

Suits/Overcoats						
American/British	36	38	40	42	44	46
Continental	46	48	50	52	54	56

Shirts				
American/British	15	16	17	18
Continental	38	41	43	45

Shoes									
American/British	5	6	7	8	8½	9	9½	10	11
Continental	38	39	41	42	43	43	44	44	45

My size is 38.	**Ik heb maat 38.**	ik hehp maat 38
I don't know the Dutch sizes.	**Ik ken de Nederlandse maten niet.**	ik kehn der nayderrlahnteer maatern neet

A good fit?

Can I try it on?	**Kan ik het aanpassen?**	kahn ik heht aanpahssern
Where's the fitting room?	**Waar is de paskamper?**	vaar iss der pahskaamerr
Is there a mirror?	**Is er een spiegel?**	iss ehr ayn speegherl
Does it fit?	**Past het?**	pahst heht

FOR NUMBERS, see page 175

It fits very well.	**Het past uitstekend.**	heht pahst ur^{ew}**t**stay**kernt**
It doesn't fit.	**Het past niet.**	heht pahst neet
It's too...	**Het is te...**	heht iss ter
short/long tight/loose	**kort/lang** **nauw/wijd**	kort/lahng noow/∀aiyt
How long will it take to alter?	**Hoe lang duurt het om het te vermaken?**	hoo lahng dewrt heht om heht ter ver**maa**kern

Shoes

I'd like a pair of...	**Ik wil graag een paar ... hebben.**	ik ∀il ghraakh ayn paar... **heh**bern
shoes/sandals boots/slippers	**schoenen/sandalen** **laarzen/pantoffels**	**skhoo**nern/sahn**daa**lern **laar**zern/pahn**tof**ferlss
These are too...	**Deze zijn te...**	**day**zer zaiyn ter
narrow/wide large/small	**nauw/wijd** **groot/klein**	no^{ow}/∀aiyt ghroat/klaiyn
They pinch my toes.	**Ze knellen aan de tenen.**	zer **kneh**lern aan der **tay**nern
Do you have a larger/smaller size?	**Hebt u een grotere/kleinere maat?**	hehpt ew ayn **ghroa**terrer/**klaiy**nerrer maat
Do you have the same in...?	**Hebt u dezelfde in het...?**	hehpt ew der**zahlf**der in heht...
brown/beige black/white	**bruin/beige** **zwart/wit**	brur^{ew}n/**beh**zher z∀ahrt/∀it
leather/rubber suede/cloth	**leer/rubber** **suède/linnen**	layr/**rur**berr se**weh**der/**lin**nern

Shoe repairs

Can you repair these shoes?	**Kunt u deze schoenen maken?**	kurnt ew **day**zer **skhoo**nern **maa**kern
Can you sew this up?	**Kunt u dit stikken?**	kurnt ew dit **sti**kkern
I'd like it/them completely resoled and heeled.	**Ik wil er graag nieuwe zolen en hakken op hebben.**	ik ∀il ehr ghraakh **nee**^{oo}∀er **zoa**lern ehn **hah**kern op **heh**bern
When will they be ready?	**Wanneer zijn ze klaar?**	∀ah**nayr** zaiyn zer klaar

Clothes and accessories

I'd like a/an/some...	**Ik wil graag ... hebben**	ik ʋil ghraakh ... **heh**bern
anorak	**een anorak**	ayn ahnoa**rahk**
blouse	**een blouse**	ayn **bloo**zer
bra	**een beha**	ayn bay**haa**
braces	**een paar bretels**	ayn paar brer**tehlss**
briefs	**een slipje**	ayn **slip**yer
cap	**een pet**	ayn peht
cardigan	**een vest**	ayn vehst
children's clothes	**kinderkleren**	**kin**derrklayrern
coat	**een jas**	ayn yahss
dinner jacket	**een smoking**	ayn **smoa**king
dress	**een jurk**	ayn yurrk
dressing gown	**een kamerjas**	ayn **kaa**merryahss
evening dress (woman's)	**een avondjurk**	ayn **aa**vontyurrk
frock	**een jurk**	ayn yurrk
fur coat	**een bontjas**	ayn **bont**yahss
garters (Am.)	**een paar jarretels**	ayn paar yahrrer**tehlss**
girdle	**een ceintuur**	ayn sehn**tewr**
gloves	**een paar handschoenen**	ayn paar **hahnt**skhoonern
handbag	**een handtas**	ayn **hahnt**tahss
handkerchief	**een zakdoek**	ayn **zahk**dook
hat	**een hoed**	ayn hoot
jacket	**een jasje**	ayn **yahs**yer
jeans	**een spijkerbroek**	ayn **spaiy**kerrbrook
jersey	**een trui**	ayn trur^{ew}
jumper	**een trui**	ayn trur^{ew}
nightdress	**een nachtjapon**	ayn **nahkht**yaapon
overalls	**een overal**	ayn oaver**rahl**
panties	**een slipje**	ayn **slip**yer
pants	**een lange broek**	ayn **lahng**er brook
pants suit	**een broekpak**	ayn **brook**pahk
panty-girdle	**een step-in broekje**	ayn steh**pin brook**yer
pyjamas	**een pyjama**	ayn pee**yaa**maa
raincoat	**een regenjas**	ayn **ray**ghernyahss
scarf	**een sjaal**	ayn shaal
shirt	**een overhemd**	ayn **oa**verrhehmt
shoes	**een paar schoenen**	ayn paar **skhoo**nern
shorts	**een short**	ayn short
skirt	**een rok**	ayn rok
slip	**een onderjurk**	ayn **on**derryurrk
socks	**een paar sokken**	ayn paar **sok**kern

sports jacket	**een sportjasje**	ayn **sport**yahssher
stockings	**een paar kousen**	ayn paar **ko^{ow}**sern
suit (man's)	**een kostuum**	ayn kos**tewm**
suit (woman's)	**een mantelpakje**	ayn **mahn**terlpahkyer
suspenders (Am.)	**een paar bretels**	ayn paar brer**tehls**
suspenders (Br.)	**een paar jarretels**	ayn paar yahrrer**tehlss**
sweater	**een trui**	ayn trur^{ew}
tie	**een stropdas**	ayn **strop**dahss
tights	**een maillot**	ayn maa**yoa**
top coat	**een overjas**	ayn **oa**verryahss
trousers	**een lange broek**	ayn **lahng**er brook
umbrella	**een paraplu**	ayn paaraa**plew**
underpants (men)	**een onderbroek**	ayn **on**derrbrook
undershirt	**een hemd**	ayn hehmt
underwear	**ondergoed**	**on**derrghoot
vest (Am.)	**een herenvest**	ayn **hay**rernvehst
vest (Br.)	**een hemd**	ayn hehmt
waistcoat	**een vest**	ayn vehst

belt	**een ceintuur**	ayn sehn**tewr**
buckle	**een gesp**	ayn ghehsp
button	**een knoop**	ayn knoap
collar	**een kraag**	ayn kraakh
elastic	**een elastiek**	ayn aylah**steek**
lining	**een voering**	ayn **voo**ring
pocket	**een zak**	ayn zahk
push-button	**een drukknoop**	ayn **drurk**-knoap
ribbon	**een lint**	ayn lint
safetypin	**een veiligheidsspeld**	ayn **vaiy**lerghhaiytsspehlt
zip (zipper)	**een ritssluiting**	ayn **rits**slur^{ew}ting

And for the beach:

bathing cap	**een badmuts**	ayn **baht**murtss
bath robe	**een badjas**	ayn **baht**yahss
straw hat	**een strohoed**	ayn **stroa**hoot
swimsuit	**een badpak**	ayn **baht**pahk
towel	**een badhanddoek**	ayn **baht**hahndook
trunks	**een zwembroek**	ayn **zvehm**brook

And for those handy with the needle:

crochet hook	**een haakpen**	ayn **haak**pehn
knitting needles	**breinaalden**	**braiy**naaldern
needle	**een naald**	ayn naalt
thimble	**een vingerhoed**	ayn **ving**errhoot
thread	**een draad**	ayn draat

Electrical appliances and accessories—Records

The standard voltage in Holland and Belgium is 220 volts A.C. However, plugs have different types of pins and you may have to get a special adaptor in order to be able to use your electrical appliances.

What's the voltage?	**Wat is de voltage?**	ʋaht iss der vol**taa**zher
I'd like an adaptor.	**Ik wil graag een verloopstekker hebben.**	ik ʋil ghraakh ayn verr**loap**stehkerr **heh**bern
Do you have a battery for this?	**Hebt u een batterij hiervoor?**	hehpt ew ayn bahter**raiy** heer**voar**
This is broken. Can you repair it?	**Dit is kapot. Kunt u het repareren?**	dit iss kaa**pot**. kurnt ew heht raypaa**ray**rern
When will it be ready?	**Wanneer is het klaar?**	ʋahnayr iss heht klaar
I'd like a/an/some...	**Ik wil graag ... hebben.**	ik ʋil ghraakh ... **heh**bern
amplifier	**een versterker**	ayn verr**stehr**kerr
battery	**een batterij**	ayn bahter**raiy**
bulb	**een (gloei)lamp**	ayn (**ghloo**$^{\bullet\bullet}$)lahmp
hair dryer	**een haardroger**	ayn **haar**droagherr
iron	**een strijkijzer**	ayn **straiy**kaiyzerr
travelling iron	**een reisstrijkijzer**	ayn **raiys**straiykaiyzerr
lamp	**een lamp**	ayn lahmp
percolator	**een koffiezetapparaat**	ayn **kof**feezehtahpaaraat
plug	**een stekker**	ayn **steh**kerr
adaptor plug	**een verloopstekker**	ayn verr**loap**stehkerr
portable ...	**een draagbare ...**	ayn **draagh**baarer
radio	**een radio**	ayn **raa**deeyoa
car radio	**een autoradio**	ayn **o**^{ow}toaraadeeyoa
record player	**een platenspeler**	ayn **plaa**ternspaylerr
shaver	**een scheerapparaat**	ayn **skhayr**ahpaaraat
speakers	**een paar luidsprekers**	ayn paar **lur**$^{\bullet ew}$tspraykerrss
tape recorder	**een bandrecorder**	ayn **bahnt**reekorderr
cassette tape recorder	**een cassetterecorder**	ayn kah**sseh**terreekorderr
television	**een televisie**	ayn tayler**vee**zee
colour television	**een kleurentelevisie**	ayn **klur**rerntaylerveezee
transformer	**een transformator**	ayn trahnsfor**maa**tor

Music shop

Do you have any records/cassettes by...?	**Hebt u platen/ cassettes van ...?**	hehpt ew plaatern/ kahssehterss vahn
Can I listen to this record/cassette?	**Kan ik deze plaat/ cassette even horen?**	kahn ik dayzer plaat/ kahssehter ayvern hoarern
I want a new stylus.	**Ik wil graag een nieuwe grammofoonnaald hebben.**	ik ʋil ghraakh ayn neeººʋer ghrahmoafoannaalt hehbern

L.P. (33 rpm)	**een langspeelplaat**	ayn lahngspaylplaat
single (45 rpm)	**een 45-toeren plaat**	ayn 45-toorern plaat
mono/stereo	**mono/stereo**	moanoa/stayreeoa

chamber music	**kamermuziek**	kaamerrmewzeek
classical music	**klassieke muziek**	klahsseeker mewzeek
folk music	**folkloristische muziek**	folkloaristeesser mewzeek
instrumental music	**instrumentale muziek**	instrewmehntaalerr mewzeek
jazz	**jazz**	jazz
light music	**lichte muziek**	likhter mewzeek
orchestral music	**orkestmuziek**	orkehstmewzeek
pop music	**popmuziek**	popmewzeek

Hairdresser's—Beauty salon

Is there a ladies' hairdresser/beauty salon in the hotel?	**Is er een dameskapper/schoonheidssalon in het hotel?**	iss ehr ayn **daa**merskahperr/ **skhoan**haiytssaalon in heht hoa**tehl**
Can I make an appointment for sometime on Thursday?	**Kan ik een afspraak voor donderdag maken?**	kahn ik ayn **ahf**spraak voar **don**derrdahkh **maa**kern
I'd like it shampooed and set.	**Ik wil het graag laten wassen en watergolven.**	ik √il heht ghraakh **laa**tern **√ah**ssern ehn **√aa**terrgholvern

in a bun	**in een knot**	in ayn knot
a cut	**geknipt**	gher**knipt**
with a fringe (bangs)	**met pony**	meht **pon**nee
a permanent wave	**met permanent**	meht pehrmaa**nehnt**
with ringlets	**met krulletjes**	meht **krur**lertyerss
a re-style	**een nieuw kapsel**	ayn nee^{oo} **kah**pserl

I want a...	**Ik wil...**	ik √il
blow-dry	**een brushing**	ayn "brushing"
colour rinse	**een kleurspoeling**	ayn **klurr**spooling
dye	**een haarverf**	ayn **haar**vehrf
setting lotion	**een haarversteviger**	ayn **haar**verrstayvergherr
shampoo for dry/ greasy/dyed hair	**shampoo voor droog/vet/ geverfd haar**	sham**poa** voar droakh/veht/ gher**vehrft** haar
touch-up	**de wortels laten bijkleuren**	der **√or**terlss **laa**tern **baiy**klurrern
Do you have a colour chart?	**Hebt u een kleurenkaart?**	hehpt ew ayn **klurr**ern-kaart
I don't want any hairspray.	**Ik wil geen haarlak.**	ik √il ghayn **haar**lahk
I want a...	**Ik wil een...**	ik √il ayn
face-pack	**gezichtsmasker**	gher**zikhts**mahskerr
manicure	**manicure**	maanee**kew**rer
pedicure	**pedicure**	**pay**deekewrer

Under the hair-dryer, you might want to say:

It's too hot.	**Het is te heet.**	heht iss ter hayt
A bit warmer/colder, please.	**Iets warmer/kouder, alstublieft.**	eets **√ahr**merr/**ko**^{ow}derr ahlstew**bleeft**

FOR TIPPING, see page 1

Barber's

I don't speak Dutch very well.	**Ik spreek niet zo goed nederlands.**	ik sprayk neet zoa ghoot **nayderrlahnts**
I'm in a hurry.	**Ik heb haast.**	ik hehp haast
I want a haircut, please.	**Ik wil graag mijn haar laten knippen.**	ik ꝟil ghraakh maiyn haar **laatern knippern**
I'd like a shave.	**Ik wil mij laten scheren.**	ik ꝟil maiy **laatern skhayrern**
Cut it short, please.	**Knipt u het kort, alstublieft.**	knipt ew heht kort ahlstew**bleeft**
Not too short.	**Niet te kort.**	neet ter kort
A razor cut, please.	**Met het mes, alstublieft.**	meht heht mehss ahlstew**bleeft**
Don't use the clippers.	**Niet met de ton-deuse, alstublieft.**	neetmeht der **tondurzer** ahlstew**bleeft**
Just a trim, please.	**Alleen bijknippen, alstublieft.**	**ahlayn baiy**knippern ahlstew**bleeft**
That's enough off.	**Zo is het kort genoeg.**	zoa iss heht kort gher**nookh**
A little more off the...	**Nog iets korter...**	nokh eets **kort**err
back	**van achteren**	vahn **akh**terrern
neck	**in de nek**	in der nehk
sides	**aan de zijkanten**	aan der **zaiy**kahntern
top	**bovenop**	**boa**vernop
I'd like a hair lotion.	**Ik wil graag haarlotion.**	ik ꝟil ghraakh een **haar**loashern
I don't want any oil.	**Ik wil geen haar-olie.**	ik ꝟil ghayn **haaroalee**
Would you please trim my...?	**Wilt u mijn ... wat bijknippen?**	ꝟilt ew maiyn ... ꝟaht **baiy**knippern
beard	**baard**	baart
moustache	**snor**	snor
sideboards (sideburns)	**bakkebaarden**	bahkerbaardern
How much do I owe you?	**Hoeveel ben ik u schuldig?**	hoova**yl** behn ik ew **skhurl**derkh
This is for you.	**Dit is voor u.**	dit iss voar ew

FOR TIPPING, see page 1

Jeweller's—Watchmaker's

Can you repair this watch?	**Kunt u dit horloge repareren?**	kurnt ew dit horloazher raypahrayrern
It's going slow/fast.	**Het loopt achter/voor.**	heht loapt **ahkh**terr/ voar
The ... is broken.	**... is kapot.**	...iss kaapot
glass	**het glas**	heht ghlass
spring	**de veer**	der vayr
strap	**het bandje**	heht **bahn**tyer
winder	**het knopje**	heht **kno**pyer
I want this watch cleaned.	**Ik wil dit horloge schoon laten maken.**	ik √il dit horloazher skhoan **laa**tern **maa**kern
When will it be ready?	**Wanneer is het klaar?**	√ahnayr iss heht klaar
Could I please see that?	**Mag ik dat even zien, alstublieft?**	mahkh ik daht ayven zeen ahlstew**bleeft**
I'm just looking around.	**Ik kijk alleen even rond.**	ik kaiyk ah**layn ay**vern ront
I want a small present for...	**Ik zoek een cadeautje voor...**	ik zook ayn kaadoatyer voar
I don't want anything too expensive.	**Het mag niet te duur zijn.**	heht mahkh neet ter dewr zaiyn
I want something...	**Ik wil iets ...**	ik √il eets
better	**beters**	**bay**terss
cheaper	**goedkopers**	ghoot**koa**perrss
simpler	**eenvoudigers**	aynvo^ow^dergherrss
Is this real silver?	**Is dit echt zilver?**	iss dit ehkht **zil**verr
Do you have anything in gold?	**Hebt u iets in goud?**	hehpt ew eets in gho^ow^t
How many carats is this?	**Hoeveel karaats is dit?**	hoo**vayl** kaa**raats** iss dit

When you go to a jeweller's, you've probably got some idea of what you want beforehand. Look up the name of the article in the following lists, then find out what it is made of.

Jewellery—Watches

I'd like a/an/some...	**Ik wil graag ... hebben.**	ik vil ghraakh ... **heh**bern
bangle	**een armring**	ayn **ahrm**ring
bracelet	**een armband**	ayn **ahrm**bahnt
brooch	**een broche**	ayn brosh
charm	**een gelukshangertje**	ayn gher**lurks**hahngerrtyer
cigarette case	**een sigarettenkoker**	ayn seeghaa**reh**ternkoakerr
cigarette lighter	**een aansteker**	ayn **aan**staykerr
clip	**een clip**	ayn klip
clock	**een klok**	ayn klok
alarm clock	**een wekker**	ayn **veh**kerr
travelling clock	**een reiswekkertje**	ayn **raiysveh**kerrtyer
collar stud	**een boordeknoop**	ayn **boar**derknoap
cross	**een kruis**	ayn krur^{ew}ss
cuff links	**een paar manchet-knopen**	ayn paar mahn**sheht**-knoapern
cutlery	**tafelzilver**	**taa**ferlzilverr
ear clips	**een paar oorbellen**	ayn paar **oar**behlern
earrings	**een paar oorbellen**	ayn paar **oar**behlern
jewel box	**een bijouteriekistje**	ayn beezhooter**ree**kistyer
manicure set	**een manicure-etui**	ayn maanee**kewrer** ay**twee**
music box	**een muziekdoos**	ayn mew**zeek**doass
napkin ring	**een servetring**	ayn sehr**veht**ring
necklace	**een halsketting**	ayn **hahls**kehting
pearl necklace	**een parelsnoer**	ayn **paa**rerlsnoor
pendant	**een hanger**	ayn **hahn**gerr
pin	**een speld**	ayn spehlt
powder compact	**een poederdoos**	ayn **poo**derrdoass
ring	**een ring**	ayn ring
diamond ring	**een diamantring**	ayn deeyaa**mahnt**ring
engagement ring	**een verlovingsring**	ayn verr**loa**vingsring
signet ring	**een zegelring**	ayn **zay**gherlring
wedding ring	**een trouwring**	ayn **tro^{ow}**ring
rosary	**een rozenkrans**	ayn **roa**zernkrahnss
silverware	**tafelzilver**	**taa**ferlzilver
snuff box	**een snuifdoos**	ayn **snur^{ew}f**doass
tie clip	**een dasclip**	ayn **dahs**klip
tie pin	**een dasspeld**	ayn **dahs**spehlt
watch	**een horloge**	ayn hor**loa**zher
pocket watch	**een zakhorloge**	ayn **zahk**horloazher
quartz watch	**een kwartshor-loge**	ayn **kvahrts**horloazher
stopwatch	**een stophorloge**	ayn **stop**horloazher
wristwatch	**een polshorloge**	ayn **pols**horloazher

watch strap	**een horlogebandje**	ayn hor**loa**zherbahntyer
chain strap	**een ketting bandje**	ayn **keh**ting **bahn**tyer
leather strap	**een leren bandje**	ayn **lay**rern **bahn**tyer
What do you call this stone?	**Hoe heet deze steen?**	hoo hayt **day**zer stayn

amber	**barnsteen**	**bahrn**stayn
amethyst	**amethist**	aamer**tist**
diamond	**diamant**	deeyaa**mahnt**
emerald	**smaragd**	smaa**rahkht**
moonstone	**maansteen**	**maan**stayn
pearl	**parel**	**paa**rerl
ruby	**robijn**	roa**baiyn**
sapphire	**saffier**	sah**feer**
tigereye	**tijgeroog**	**taiy**gherroakh
topaz	**topaas**	**toa**paas
turquoise	**turkoois**	**turr**koa^{ee}ss

What's it made of?	**Waar is het van gemaakt?**	**v**aar iss heht vahn gher**maakt**

alabaster	**albast**	ahl**bahst**
brass	**geel koper**	ghayl **koa**perr
bronze	**brons**	bronss
chromium	**chroom**	ghroam
copper	**koper**	**koa**perr
coral	**koraal**	koa**raal**
crystal	**kristal**	kris**tahl**
ebony	**ebbenhout**	**eh**bernho^{ow}t
enamel	**emaille**	ay**mah**yer
glass	**glas**	ghlahss
cut glass	**geslepen glas**	gher**slay**pern ghlahss
gold	**goud**	gho^{ow}t
gold plate	**verguld**	verr**ghurlt**
ivory	**ivoor**	ee**voar**
jade	**jade**	**yaa**der
mother-of-pearl	**paarlemoer**	**paar**lermoor
pearl	**parel**	**paa**rerl
pewter	**tin**	tin
platinum	**platina**	**plaa**teenaa
silver	**zilver**	**zil**verr
silver plate	**verzilverd**	verr**zil**verrt
stainless steel	**roestvrij staal**	**roost**vraiy staal

Laundry—Dry cleaning

If your hotel doesn't have its own laundry or dry-cleaning service, ask the hotel receptionist:

Where's the nearest...?	**Waar is de dichtstbijzijnde...?**	vaar iss der dikhtst-baiy**zaiy**nder
dry cleaner's	**stomerij**	stoamer**raiy**
launderette	**wasserette**	vahsser**reh**ter
laundry	**wasserij**	vahsser**raiy**
I want these clothes...	**Ik wil deze kleren laten...**	ik vil **day**zer **klay**rern **laa**tern
cleaned	**stomen**	**stoa**mern
ironed	**strijken**	**straiy**kern
pressed	**persen**	**peh**rsern
washed	**wassen**	**vah**ssern
When will it be ready?	**Wanneer zijn ze klaar?**	vahn**nayr** zaiyn zer klaar
I need it...	**Ik heb ze ... nodig**	ik hehp zer ... **noa**derkh
today	**vandaag**	vahn**daakh**
tonight	**vanavond**	vahn**aa**vont
tomorrow	**morgen**	**mor**ghern
before Friday	**vóór vrijdag**	**voar vraiy**dahkh
Can you ... this?	**Kunt u dit...?**	kurnt ew dit
mend	**repareren**	raypaa**ray**rern
patch	**verstellen**	verr**steh**lern
sew	**naaien**	**naa**yern
Can you sew on this button?	**Kunt u deze knoop aanzetten?**	kurnt ew **day**zer knoap **aan**zehtern
Can you get this stain out?	**Kunt u deze vlek verwijderen?**	kurnt ew **day**zer vlehk verr**vaiy**derrern
Can this be invisibly mended?	**Kan dit onzichtbaar gestopt worden?**	kahn dit on**zikht**baar gher**stopt vor**dern
This isn't mine.	**Dit is niet van mij.**	dit iss neet vahn maiy
Is my laundry ready?	**Is mijn was klaar?**	iss maiyn vahss klaar?
You promised it for today.	**U had het mij voor vandaag beloofd.**	ew haht heht maiy voar vahn**daakh** ber**loaft**

FOR DAYS OF THE WEEK, see page 181

Photography

I want an inexpensive camera.	**Ik wil een goedkoop fototoestel.**	ik √il ayn ghoot**koap** **foa**toatoostehl
Do you sell cine (movie) cameras?	**Verkoopt u filmtoestellen?**	verr**koapt** ew **fil**mtoostehlern
May I have a prospectus?	**Mag ik een prospectus van u hebben?**	mahkh ik ayn pros**pehk**turss vahn ew **heh**bern
I would like to have some passport photos taken.	**Ik zou graag wat paspoortfoto's willen laten maken.**	ik zoᵒʷ ghraakh √aht **pahs**poartfoatoass **√i**llern **laa**tern **maa**kern

Film

Film sizes aren't always indicated the same way in Europe as in the United States and Great Britain. Listed below you'll find some equivalents and translations.

I'd like a film for this camera.	**Ik wil graag een film voor dit toestel.**	ik √il ghraakh ayn film voar dit **too**stehl
black-and-white film	**een zwart-wit film**	ayn z√art-√it film
colour film	**een kleurenfilm**	ayn **klur**rernfilm
colour slides	**een diarolletje**	ayn **dee**yaarolertyer
cartridge	**een kardoes**	ayn kahr**dooss**
cassette	**een cassette**	ayn kah**sseh**ter
roll of film	**een rolletje film**	ayn **ro**lertyer film
120	**een zes bij zes film**	ayn zehss baiy zehss film
127	**een vier bij vier film**	ayn veer baiy veer film
135	**een vierentwintig bij zesendertig film**	ayn veerehnt**√in**terkh baiy zehsehn**dehr**terkh film
8 mm	**een acht-millimeter film**	ayn ahkht**mee**leemayterr film
super 8	**een super-acht**	ayn **sew**perr ahkht
20/36 exposures	**met twintig/zesendertig opnamen**	meht **t√in**terkh/zehsehn**dehr**terkh **op**naamern
this ASA/DIN number	**met dit ASA/DIN nummer**	meht dit aa-ehss-aa/din **nur**merr
artificial light type	**voor kunstlicht**	voar **kurnst**likht
daylight type	**voor daglicht**	voar **dahgh**likht
fast	**snel**	snehl
fine grain	**fijnkorrelig**	faiyn**kor**rerlerkh

Processing

How much do you charge for developing?	**Hoeveel kost het ontwikkelen?**	hoovayl kost heht ontʋikkerlern
I want ... prints of each negative.	**Ik wil graag ... afdrukken van elk negatief.**	ik ʋil ghraakh ... ahfdrurkkern vahn ehlker nayghaa**teef**
Will you please enlarge this?	**Wilt u dit vergroten, alstublieft?**	ʋilt ew dit verr**ghroa**tern ahlstew**bleeft**
mat/glossy finish	**een matte/glanzende afdruk**	ayn **mah**tter/**ghlahn**zernder **ahf**drurk
with/without border	**met/zonder rand**	meht/**zon**derr rahnt

Accessories

I want a/some ...	**Ik wil graag ...**	ik ʋil ghraakh
filter	**een filter**	ayn **fil**terr
red/yellow	**rode/gele**	roader/ghayler
ultraviolet	**ultra-violette**	urltraa-veeyoa**leh**ter
flash bulbs	**een paar flitslampjes**	ayn paar **flits**lahmpyerss
flash cubes	**een paar flitskubes**	ayn paar **flits**kewberss
lens	**een lens**	ayn lehnss
lens cap	**een lensdop**	ayn **lehns**dop
light meter	**een belichtingsmeter**	ayn ber**likh**tinghsmayterr
telephoto lens	**een telefoto lens**	ayn taylay**foa**toa lehnss

Repairs

Can you repair this camera?	**Kunt u dit fototoestel repareren?**	kurnt ew dit **foa**toa-toostehl raypaa**ray**rern
The film is jammed.	**De film draait niet door.**	der film draa**eet** neet doar
There's something wrong with the ...	**Er hapert iets aan ...**	ehr **haa**perrt eets aan
exposure counter	**de opnameteller**	der opnaamer**teh**lerr
film winder	**de terugspoelknop**	der terrurghspoolknop
light meter	**de belichtingsmeter**	der ber**likh**tinghsmayterr
rangefinder	**de afstandsmeter**	der **ahf**stahntsmayterr
shutter	**de sluiter**	der **slur^{ew}**terr
Could you make an estimate, please?	**Kunt u mij een prijsopgave geven, alstublieft?**	kurnt ew maiy ayn **praiyss**-opghaaver **ghay**vern ahlstew**bleeft**

Provisions

Here's a basic list of food and drink that you might want on a picnic or for the occasional meal in your hotel room.

I'd like a/an/some...	**Ik wil graag ... van u hebben.**	ik √il ghraakh ... vahn ew **heh**bern
apple juice	**appelsap**	**ah**perlsahp
apples	**appels**	**ah**perlss
bananas	**bananen**	baa**naa**nern
beer	**bier**	beer
biscuits (Br.)	**beschuitjes**	ber**skhur**ᵉʷtyerss
bread	**een brood**	ayn broat
butter	**boter**	**boa**terr
cheese	**kaas**	kaass
(grilled) chicken	**een (gebakken) kip**	ayn (gher**bah**kern) kip
chocolate	**chocolade**	shoakoa**laa**der
coffee	**koffie**	**kof**fee
instant coffee	**instant koffie**	**in**stahnt **kof**fee
cold cuts	**vleeswaren**	**vlays**√aarern
cookies	**koekjes**	**kook**yerss
cream	**room**	roam
cucumber	**een komkommer**	ayn kom**kom**merr
eggs	**eieren**	**ai**yyerrern
frankfurters	**knakworstjes**	**knahk**√orstyerss
gherkins	**augurken**	oᵒʷ**ghurr**kern
grapefruit	**pompelmoes**	**pom**perlmooss
grapefruit juice	**pompelmoessap**	**pom**perlmoossahp
ham	**ham**	hahm
hamburgers	**hamburgers**	**hahm**burrgherrss
ice-cream	**ijs**	aiyss
lemons	**citroenen**	see**troo**nern
lettuce	**sla**	slaa
liver sausage	**leverworst**	**lay**verr√orst
milk	**melk**	mehlk
mineral water	**mineraalwater**	meenerr**aal**√aaterr
mustard	**mosterd**	**mos**terrt
(olive) oil	**(olijf)olie**	(oa**laiyf**)oalee
oranges	**sinaasappels**	**see**naasahperlss
orange juice	**sinaasappelsap**	**see**naasahperlssahp
pepper	**peper**	**pay**perr
potato crisps (chips)	**chips**	"chips"
potatoes	**aardappels**	**aar**dahperlss
rolls	**broodjes**	**broa**tyerss
salad	**sla**	slaa
salami	**salami**	saa**laa**mee

salt	**zout**	zo^{ow}t
sandwich	**een sandwich**	ayn "sandwich"
sausage	**een worst**	ayn vorst
soft drink	**limonade**	leemoanaader
soup	**soep**	soop
spices	**specerijen**	spayserraiyyern
sugar	**suiker**	sur^{ew}kerr
sweets	**snoep**	snoop
tea	**thee**	tay
tea bags	**theezakjes**	tayzahkyerss
tomatoes	**tomaten**	toamaatern
tomato juice	**tomatensap**	toamaaternsahp
wine	**wijn**	vaiyn
yoghurt	**joghurt**	yokhurrt

And don't forget:

a bottle opener	**een flesopener**	ayn **flehss**oapernerr
a corkscrew	**een kurketrekker**	ayn **kurr**kertrehkerr
matches	**lucifers**	**lew**sseefehrss
(paper) napkins	**(papieren) servetjes**	(paa**pee**rern) sehr**veht**yerss
a tin (can) opener	**een blikopener**	ayn **blik**oapernerr

basket	**een mand**	ayn mahnd
bottle	**een fles**	ayn flehss
box	**een doos**	ayn doass
carton	**een karton**	ayn kahr**ton**
glass	**een glas**	ayn ghlahss
packet	**een pakje**	ayn **pah**kyer
plastic bag	**een plastik zakje**	ayn **pleh**steek **zah**kyer
tube	**een tube**	ayn **tew**ber

Weights and measures

1 kilogram or kilo (kg) = 1000 grams (g)

100 g = 3.5 oz.	½ kg = 1.1 lb.
200 g = 7.0 oz.	1 kg = 2.2 lb.

1 oz. = 28.35 g
1 lb. = 453.60 g

1 litre (l) = 0.88 imp. quarts = 1.06 U.S. quarts

1 imp. quart = 1.14 l	1 U.S. quart = 0.95 l
1 imp. gallon = 4.55 l	1 U.S. gallon = 3.8 l

S... ...irs

The best-known Dutch souvenirs include costumed dolls wooden shoes and blue pottery from Delft. Authentic Delft pottery also comprises white, red and multicoloured ceramics. Other high-quality products of Dutch arts and crafts are cut diamonds from Amsterdam, glass and crystal from Leerdam and silverware from Schoonhoven. In Belgium, you should look for lace, crystal and porcelain.

bulbs	**bloembollen**	**bloom**bollern
cast-iron casseroles	**gietijzeren potten**	**ghee**taiyzerrern **po**ttern
copperware	**koperwaren**	**koa**perrvaarern
crystal	**kristal**	kris**tahl**
Delft earthenware	**Delfts aardewerk**	**deh**lfts **aar**dervahrk
diamonds (cut)	**diamanten (geslepen)**	deeyaa**mahn**tern (gher**slay**pern)
dolls in local costumes	**poppen in klederdracht**	poppern in **klay**derrdrahkht
glass	**glas**	ghlahss
lace	**kant**	kahnt
pewter	**tin**	tin
silverware	**tafelzilver**	**taa**ferlzilverr
tapestry	**een wandtapijt**	ayn **vahnt**taapaiyt
wood carvings	**gesneden houten voorwerpen**	ghers**nay**dern **ho**ʷtern **voar**vehrpern
wooden shoes (clogs)	**een paar klompen**	ayn paar **klom**pern

It may be best not to take bulbs out of the country yourself, since customs regulations concerning plants and bulbs are quite complex. However, Dutch flower bulb dealers are fully conversant with legal provisions and arrange shipments of bulbs all over the world.

There are also many typical Dutch sweets (candies) and items of confectionery you might wish to take back with you. Children will love *chocoladehagelslag*—shoakoa**laa**der**haag**herlslahkh (chocolate) on their bread. The spiced cakes from Groningen and Deventer as well as the Frisian *kruidkoek* are a real delight. And, finally, *Haagse hopjes* are considered the most famous of all Dutch sweets.

SHOPPING GUIDE

Tobacconist's

Cigarettes and tobacco are sold in *sigarenwinkels* (tobacconists'), supermarkets and a street kiosks.

As at home, cigarettes are generally referred to by their brand names. English and American cigarettes are available, but cigarettes produced in the Benelux countries (Holland, Belgium and Luxembourg) under special licence are very similar to American brands.

Give me a/some ..., please.	**Geeft u me ..., alstublieft.**	ghayft ew mer ... ahlstewbleeft
chewing tobacco	**pruimtabak**	prur^{ew}mtaabahk
cigars	**een paar sigaren**	ayn paar seeghaarern
box of cigars	**een doosje sigaren**	ayn doasyer seeghaarern
cigarette case	**een sigarettenkoker**	ayn seeghaarehternkoakerr
cigarette holder	**een sigarettepijpje**	ayn seeghaarehterpaiypyer
cigarette lighter	**een sigaretten-aansteker**	ayn seeghaarehtern-aanstaykerr
cigarette paper	**sigarettenpapier**	seeghaarehternpaapeer
cigarettes	**sigaretten**	seeghaarehtern
packet of cigarettes	**een pakje sigaretten**	ayn pahkyer seeghaarehtern
flints	**wat vuursteentjes**	vaht vewrstayntyerss
lighter	**een aansteker**	ayn aanstaykerr
lighter fluid/gas	**benzine/gas voor een aansteker**	behnzeener/ghahss voar ayn aanstaykerr
matches	**lucifers**	lewsseefehrss
pipe	**een pijp**	ayn paiyp
pipe cleaners	**pijpestokers**	paiyperstoakerrss
pipe rack	**een pijpenrek**	ayn paiypernrehk
pipe tobacco	**wat pijptabak**	vaht paiyptaabahk
pipe tool	**een pijpestopper**	ayn paiyperstoakerrtyer
refill for a lighter	**een vulling voor een aansteker**	ayn vurling voar ayn aanstaykerr
snuff	**snuiftabak**	snur^{ew}ftaabahk
tobacco pouch	**een tabaksbuil**	ayn taabahksbur^{ew}l
wick	**een lont**	ayn lont
Do you have any...?	**Hebt u...?**	hehpt ew
American/English cigarettes	**Amerikaanse/ Engelse sigaretten**	aamayreekaansser/ ehngerlsser seeghaarehtern
menthol cigarettes	**menthol sigaretten**	mehntol seeghaarehtern

I'll take two packets.	**Twee pakjes, alstublieft.**	tʋay **pah**kyers ahlstew**bleeft**
I'd like a carton.	**Een slof, alstublieft.**	ayn sloff ahlstew**bleeft**
A box of matches, please.	**Een doosje lucifers, alstublieft.**	ayn **doas**yer **lew**sseefehrss ahlstew**bleeft**

filter tipped	**met filter**	meht **fil**terr
without filter	**zonder filter**	**zon**derr **fil**terr
light tobacco	**lichte tabak**	**likh**ter taa**bahk**
dark tobacco	**donkere tabak**	**don**kerrer taa**bahk**

While we're on the subject of cigarettes:

Would you like a cigarette?	**Wilt u een sigaret?**	ʋilt ew ayn seeghaa**reht**
Have one of mine.	**Neemt u er een van mij.**	naymt ew ehr ayn vahn maiy
Try one of these. They're very mild.	**Probeert u deze eens. Ze zijn heel licht.**	proa**bayrt** ew **day**zer aynss. zer zaiyn hayl likht
They're a bit strong.	**Ze zijn tamelijk zwaar.**	zer zaiyn **taa**merlerk zʋaar

And if somebody offers you one?

Thank you.	**Dank u wel**	dahnk ew ʋehl
No, thanks.	**Nee, dank u.**	nay dahnk
I don't smoke.	**Ik rook niet.**	ik roak neet
I've given it up.	**Ik rook niet meer.**	ik roak neet mayr

ROKEN
SMOKERS

ROKEN VERBODEN
NO SMOKING

Your money: banks—currency

In Holland banks are open from 9 a.m. to 4 p.m., Monday to Friday, and sometimes in the evening too. The basic unit of currency in Holland is the *gulden*—**ghurl**dern (guilder), abbreviated to *f, fl* or, especially outside the country, *Hfl.* A guilder is divided into 100 *centen*—**sehn**tern (cents), Here are the different types of coins in circulation:

5 cents	**een stuiver**	ayn stur^{ew}verr
10 cents	**een dubbeltje**	ayn durberltyer
25 cents	**een kwartje**	ayn kvahrtyer
1 guilder	**een gulden**	ayn ghurldern
2.50 guilders	**een rijksdaalder**	ayn raiyksdaalderr

The different types of banknotes are:

5 guilders	**vijf gulden**	vaiyf ghurldern
10 guilders	**tien gulden**	teen ghurldern
25 guilders	**vijfentwintig gulden**	vaiyfehntvinterkh ghurldern
50 guilders	**vijftig gulden**	vaiyfterkh ghurldern
100 guilders	**honderd gulden**	honderrt ghurldern
1,000 guilders	**duizend gulden**	dur^{ew}zernt ghurldern

In Belgium the basic unit of currency is the *franc* (frahnk), divided into 100 *centimes* (sahn**tee**mern). There are coins of 50 centimes, 1, 5, 10 and 20 francs and banknotes of 50, 100, 500, 1,000 and 5,000 francs. Banks are open from 9 a.m. to 12.30 and from 2.30 p.m. to 3.30 p.m. (sometimes from 9 a.m. to 4 p.m.), Monday to Friday.

Where's the nearest bank/currency exchange?	**Waar is de dichtstbijzijnde bank/het wisselkantoor?**	vaar iss der dikhtst-baiyzaiynder bahnk/heht visserlkahntoar

Where can I cash a traveller's cheque (check)?	**Waar kan ik een reischeque inwisselen?**	∀aar kahn ik ayn **raiys**shehks in **∀**isserlern
I want to change some dollars/pounds.	**Ik wil graag wat dollars/ponden wisselen.**	ik ∀il ghraakh ∀aht **do**llahrss/**pon**dern **∀**isserlern
What's the exchange rate?	**Wat is de wissel-koers?**	∀aht iss der **∀**isserlkoorss
What rate of commission do you charge?	**Hoeveel provisie berekent u?**	hoo**vayl** proa**vee**see ber**ray**kernt ew
Can you cash a personal cheque?	**Neemt u cheques aan?**	naymt ew shehks aan
Here's my passport.	**Hier is mijn pas-poort.**	heer iss maiyn **pahs**poart
How long will it take to clear?	**Hoe lang duurt de verificatie?**	hoo lahng dewrt der vayreefee**kaat**see
Can you wire my bank in London?	**Kunt u naar mijn bank in London telegraferen?**	kurnt ew naar maiyn bahnk in **lon**dern taylerghraa**fay**rern
I have...	**Ik heb...**	ik hehp
a letter of credit	**een kredietbrief**	ayn krer**deet**breef
an introduction from...	**een introduktiebrief van...**	ayn introa**durk**seebreef vahn
a credit card	**een kredietkaart**	ayn krer**deet**kaart
I'm expecting some money from New York.	**Ik verwacht geld uit New York.**	ik verr**∀ahkht** ghehlt ur^{ew}t "new york"
Has it arrived yet?	**Is het al aange-komen?**	iss heht ahl **aan**gherkoamern
Please give me... notes (bills) and some small denomi-nations.	**Geeft u mij ... biljet-ten en wat kleingeld, alstublieft.**	ghayft ew maiy ... bil**yeh**tern ehn ∀aht klaiyn**ghelt** ahlstew**bleeft**
Give me ... large notes and the rest in small notes.	**Geeft u mij ... in grote coupures en de rest in kleine cou-pures, alstublieft.**	ghayft ew maiy ... in **ghroa**ter koo**pew**rerss ehn der rehst in **klaiy**ner koo**pew**rerss ahlstew**bleeft**
Could you please check that again?	**Kunt u dat nog eens controleren, alstublieft?**	kurnt ew daht nokh aynss kontroa**lay**rern ahlstew**bleeft**

Depositing

I want to credit this to my account.	**Ik wil dit geld op mijn rekening storten.**	ik √il dit ghehlt op maiyn raykerning stortern
I want to credit this to Mr. ...'s account.	**Ik wil dit graag op de rekening van de Heer ... storten.**	ik √il dit ghraakh op der raykerning vahn der hayr stortern
Where should I sign?	**Waar moet ik tekenen?**	√aar moot ik taykernern

Currency converter

In a world of floating currencies, we can offer no more than this do-it-yourself chart. You can get a card showing current exchange rates from banks and travel agents.

	£	$
10 cents		
25 cents		
1 guilder		
10 guilders		
50 guilders		
100 guilders		
500 guilders		
1000 guilders		
10 Belgian francs		
50 Belgian francs		
100 Belgian francs		
250 Belgian francs		
500 Belgian francs		
1000 Belgian francs		

FOR NUMBERS, see page 175

At the post office

In Holland, post offices can be recognized by the letters *PTT (Post, Telegraaf, Telefoon).* They are generally open from Monday to Friday between 8.30 a.m. and 5 p.m. On Saturdays, some post offices are open from 8.30 a.m. to noon. In Belgium opening hours are from 9 a.m. to 5 p.m.

Mailboxes *(brievenbussen)* in Holland are painted grey and red, while they are red in Belgium. The hours when mail is picked up are noted on the mailbox.

Where is the nearest post office?	**Waar is het dichtstbijzijnde postkantoor?**	√aar iss heht dikhtst-baiy**zaiyn**der **post**kahntoar
What time does the post office open/close?	**Hoe laat gaat het postkantoor open/dicht?**	hoo laat ghaat heht **post**kahntoar **oa**pern/dikht
What window do I go to for stamps?	**Aan welk loket moet ik zijn voor postzegels?**	aan √ehlk loa**keht** moot ik zaiyn voar **post**zaygherlss
At which counter can I cash an international money order?	**Aan welk loket kan ik een internationale postwissel innen?**	aan √ehlk loa**keht** kahn ik ayn interrnahsyo**naa**ler **post**√isserl innern
I want some stamps.	**Ik wil een paar postzegels.**	ik √il ayn paar **post**zaygherlss
I want ... 30-cent stamps and ... 50-cent stamps.	**Ik wil graag ... postzegels van 30 cent en ... postzegels van 50 cent.**	if √il ghraakh ... **post**zaygherlss vahn 30 sehnt ehn ... **post**zaygherlss van 50 sehnt
What is the postage for a letter to Great Britain?	**Hoeveel moet er op een brief naar Engeland?**	hoo**vayl** moot ehr op ayn breef naar **ehng**erlahnt
What is the postage for a postcard to the U.S.A.?	**Hoeveel moet er op een briefkaart naar de Verenigde Staten?**	hoo**vayl** moot ehr op ayn **breef**kaart naar der verraynerghder **staa**tern
Do all letters go airmail?	**Gaan alle brieven per luchtpost?**	ghaan **ah**ler **bree**vern pehr **lurkht**post

I want to send this parcel.	**Ik wil graag dit pakje versturen.**	ik ꝟil ghraakh dit **pah**kyer verr**stew**rern
Where's the mailbox?	**Waar is de brievenbus?**	ꝟaar iss der **bree**vernburss
I want to send this by ...	**Ik wil dit graag ... versturen.**	ik ꝟil dit ghraakh ... verr**stew**rern
airmail	**per luchtpost**	pehr **lurkht**post
express (special delivery)	**per expresse**	pehr ehks**prehss**
registered mail	**aangetekend**	**aan**ghertaykernt
Where's the poste restante (general delivery)?	**Waar is de poste restante?**	ꝟaar iss der **pos**ter reh**stahn**ter
Is there any mail for me? My name is ...	**Is er post voor mij? Mijn naam is ...**	iss ehr post voar maiy? maiyn naam iss

POSTZEGELS	STAMPS
PAKJES	PARCELS
POSTWISSELS	MONEY ORDERS

Telegrams

Cables and telegrams are dispatched by the post office.

I want to send a telegram. May I have a form?	**Ik wil graag een telegram versturen. Mag ik een formulier, alstublieft?**	ik ꝟil ghraakh ayn tayler**ghrahm** verr**stew**rern. mahgh ik ayn formew**leer** ahlstew**bleeft**
How much is it per word?	**Hoeveel kost het per woord?**	hoo**vayl** kost heht pehr ꝟoart
How long will a cable to Boston take?	**Hoe lang doet een telegram naar Boston erover?**	hoo lahng doot ayn tayler**ghrahm** naar **bos**tern ehr**oa**verr
I'd like to reverse the charges.	**Ik wil het graag door de geadresseerde laten betalen.**	ik ꝟil heht ghraakh doar der gheraadreh**ssayr**der **laa**tern ber**taa**lern
I'd like to send a night-letter.	**Ik zou graag een brief-telegram willen versturen.**	ik zo^{ow} ghraakh ayn breef-tayler**ghrahm** **ꝟil**lern verr**stew**rern

Telephoning

The telephone system is fully automatic in both Holland and Belgium, and direct calls can be made to most places in the world providing you have the correct prefix number of the relevant country and the area or dialling code (*netnummer*—**neht**nurmerr). Rates are considerably cheaper for long-distance calls made between 6 p.m. and 8 p.m. and during the weekend from 6 p.m. on Friday until 8 a.m. on Monday. Long-distance calls can be made from most telephone booths and all post offices. All public phones list directions for use in English.

General

Where's the telephone?	**Waar is de telefoon?**	ʋaar iss der taylerfoan
Where's the nearest telephone booth?	**Waar is de dichtstbijzijnde telefooncel?**	ʋaar iss der dikhtst-baiyzaiynder tayler-foansehl
Could you give me some small change for the telephone?	**Kunt u mij wat kleingeld geven voor de telefoon?**	kurnt ew maiy ʋaht klaiyn-ghehlt ghayvern voar der taylerfoan
May I use your telephone?	**Mag ik uw telefoon even gebruiken?**	mahkh ik ewʋ taylerfoan ayvern gherbrur[ew]kern
Do you have a telephone directory for Amsterdam?	**Hebt u een telefoonboek van Amsterdam?**	hehpt ew ayn taylerfoan-book vahn ahmsterrdahm
Can you help me get this number?	**Kunt u mij helpen om dit nummer te bereiken?**	kurnt ew maiy hehlpern om dit nurmerr ter berraiy-kern

Operator

Do you speak English?	**Spreekt u Engels?**	spraykt ew ehngerlss
Good morning, I want Amsterdam 123456.	**Goede morgen, ik wil graag nummer 123456 in Amsterdam.**	ghooder morghern ik ʋil ghraakh nurmerr 123456 in ahmsterrdahm

FOR NUMBERS, see page 175

I want to place a personal (person-to-person) call.	**Ik wil graag een gesprek met voorbericht.**	ik ∀il ghraakh ayn ghe**sprehk** meht **voar**-berrikht
I want to reverse the charges.	**Ik wil telefoneren op kosten van de ontvanger.**	ik ∀il taylerfoanayrern op **kos**tern vahn der ont**vahng**err

Speaking

Hello. This is ... speaking.	**Hallo. U spreekt met ...**	hah**loa**. ew spraykt meht
I want to speak to ...	**Ik wil graag ... spreken.**	ik ∀il ghraakh ... **spray**kern
I want extension ...	**Ik wil graag nummer ...**	ik ∀il ghraakh **nur**merr
Is that ...?	**Spreek ik met ...?**	sprayk ik meht

Bad luck

Operator, you gave me the wrong number.	**Juffrouw, u hebt mij verkeerd verbonden.**	yurfro^{ow} ew hehpt maiy verr**kayrt** verr**bon**dern
Operator, we were cut off.	**Juffrouw, de telefoonverbinding werd verbroken.**	yurfro^{ow} der taylerfoanverrbinding ∀ehrt verr**broa**kern

Telephone alphabet

A	**Anna**	ahnaa	O	**Otto**	ottoa
B	**Bernard**	behrnahrt	P	**Pieter**	peeterr
C	**Cornelis**	kornayliss	Q	**Quadraat**	k∀aadraat
D	**Dirk**	dirk	R	**Rudolf**	rewdolf
E	**Eduard**	aydewahrt	S	**Simon**	seemon
F	**Ferdinand**	fehrdeenant	T	**Teunis**	tur^{ew}niss
G	**Gerard**	ghayrahrt	U	**Utrecht**	ewtrehkht
H	**Hendrik**	hehndrik	V	**Victor**	viktor
I	**Izaak**	eezahk	W	**Willem**	∀illerm
J	**Jan**	yahn	X	**Xantippe**	ksahntipper
K	**Karel**	kaarerl	IJ	**IJmuiden**	aiymur^{ew}dern
L	**Lodewijk**	loader∀aiyk	Y	**Ypsilon**	eepserlon
M	**Marie**	maaree	Z	**Zaandam**	zaandahm
N	**Nico**	neeko			

The connexion was bad.	**De verbinding was slecht.**	der verr**binding** √ahss slehkht
Would you please try the number again?	**Wilt u dit nummer nog eens proberen, alstublieft?**	√ilt ew dit **nur**merr nokh ayns proa**bay**rern ahlstew**bleeft**

Not there

When will he/she be back?	**Wanneer komt hij/zij terug?**	√ahn**ayr** komt haiy/zaiy ter**rurkh**
Will you tell him/her I called? My name is...	**Wilt u hem/haar zeggen dat ik gebeld heb. Mijn naam is...**	√ilt ew hehm/haar **zeh**ghern daht ik gher**behlt** hehp. maiyn naam iss
Would you ask him/her to call me?	**Wilt u hem/haar vragen mij terug te bellen?**	√ilt ew hehm/haar **vraa**ghern maiy ter**rurgh** ter **beh**lern
Would you please take a message?	**Wilt u een boodschap doorgeven, alstublieft?**	√ilt ew ayn **boat**skhahp **doar**ghayvern ahlstew**bleeft**

Charges

What was the cost of that call?	**Hoeveel heeft dit gesprek gekost?**	hoo**vayl** hayft dit gher**sprehk** gher**kost**
I want to pay for the call.	**Ik wil graag het gesprek betalen.**	ik √il ghraakh heht gher**sprehk** ber**taa**lern

Er is telefoon voor u.	There's a telephone call for you.
Welk nummer belt u?	What number are you calling?
De lijn is bezet.	The line is engaged.
Er is geen gehoor.	There's no answer.
U bent verkeerd verbonden.	You've got the wrong number.
De telefoon is defekt.	The telephone is out of order.
Hij/Zij is er momenteel niet.	He's/She's out at the moment.
Zal ik het later nog eens proberen?	Shall I try again later?

The car

Filling stations

We'll start this section by considering your possible needs at a filling station. Most of them don't handle major repairs; but apart from providing you with fuel, they may be helpful in solving all kinds of minor problems.

Where's the nearest filling station?	**Waar is het dichtstbijzijnde benzinestation?**	ʋaar iss heht dikhtst-baiyzaiynder behnzeener-staasyon
I want 20 litres of petrol (gas), please.	**Twintig liter benzine, alstublieft.**	tʋinterkh **lee**terr behnzeener ahlstew**bleeft**
Give me ... guilders' worth of standard/premium.	**Voor ... gulden normaal/super.**	voar ... **ghurl**dern normaal/sooperr
Fill it up, please.	**Vol, alstublieft.**	vol ahlstew**bleeft**
Please check the oil and water.	**Controleert u de olie en het water even, alstublieft?**	kontroa**layrt** ew der **oa**lee ehn heht **ʋaa**terr **ay**vern ahlstew**bleeft**
Give me half a litre of oil.	**Een halve liter olie, alstublieft.**	ayn **hahl**ver **lee**terr **oa**lee ahlstew**bleeft**
Fill up the battery with distilled water.	**Vult u de accu even bij met gedistilleerd water.**	vurlt ew der **ah**kew **ay**vern baiy meht gherdistee**layrt ʋaa**terr
Check the brake fluid.	**Controleert u de remvloeistof even, alstublieft?**	kontroa**layrt** ew der **rehm**-vloo[ee]stof **ay**vern ahlstew**bleeft**

Fluid measures					
litres	imp. gal.	U.S. gal.	litres	imp. gal.	U.S. gal.
5	1.1	1.3	30	6.6	7.8
10	2.2	2.6	35	7.7	9.1
15	3.3	3.9	40	8.8	10.4
20	4.4	5.2	45	9.9	11.7
25	5.5	6.5	50	11.0	13.0

FOR NUMBERS, see page 175

Would you check the tire pressure?	**Wilt u de banden even controleren, alstublieft?**	ʋilt ew der **bahn**dern **ay**vern kontroa**lay**rern ahlstew**bleeft**
1.6 front, 1.8 rear.	**Vóór 1 komma 6 en achter 1 komma 8.**	**voar** ayn **ko**mmaa zehss ehn **ahkh**terr ayn **ko**mmaa ahkht
Please check the spare tire, too.	**Controleert u ook even het reserve-wiel, alstublieft.**	kontroa**layrt** ew ook **ay**vern heht rer**sehr**verʋeel ahlstew**bleeft**
Can you mend this puncture (fix this flat)?	**Kunt u deze lekke band repareren?**	kurnt ew **day**zer **leh**ker bahnt raypaa**ray**rern
Would you please change this tire?	**Wilt u deze band verwisselen, alstublieft?**	ʋilt ew **day**zer bahnt verr**ʋi**sserlern ahlstew**bleeft**
Would you clean the windscreen (windshield)?	**Wilt u de voorruit schoonmaken, alstublieft?**	ʋilt ew der **voar**rur^ew^t **skhoan**maakern ahlstew**bleeft**
Have you a road map of this district?	**Hebt u een wegenkaart van deze streek?**	hehpt ew ayn **ʋay**ghernkaart vahn **day**zer strayk
Where are the toilets?	**Waar zijn de toiletten?**	ʋaar zaiyn der tʋaa**leh**tern

Tire pressure is measured in Holland in kilograms per square centimetre. The following conversion chart will make sure your tires get the treatment they deserve.

Tire pressure

lb./sq. in.	kg./cm²	lb./sq. in.	kg./cm²
10	0.7	26	1.8
12	0.8	27	1.9
15	1.1	28	2.0
18	1.3	30	2.1
20	1.4	33	2.3
21	1.5	36	2.5
23	1.6	38	2.7
24	1.7	40	2.8

Asking the way—Street directions

Excuse me.	**Neemt u mij niet kwalijk.**	naymt ew maiy neet kꝞaalerk
Do you speak English?	**Spreekt u Engels?**	spraykt ew **ehn**gerlss
Can you tell me the way to ...?	**Kunt u mij de weg wijzen naar ...?**	kurnt ew maiy der Ꝟahkh Ꝟaiyzern naar
Where's ...	**Waar is ...?**	Ꝟaar iss
How do I get to ...?	**Hoe kom ik naar ...?**	hoo kom ik naar
Where does this road lead to?	**Waar gaat deze weg heen?**	Ꝟaar ghaat **day**zer Ꝟehkh hayn
Are we on the right road for...?	**Zitten we op de goeie weg naar...?**	**zit**tern Ꝟer op der **ghoo**yer Ꝟehkh naar
How far is the next village?	**Hoever is het volgende dorp?**	hoo**vehr** iss heht **vol**ghernder dorp
How far is it to ... from here?	**Hoever is het van hier naar ...?**	hoo**vehr** iss heht vahn heer naar
Can you tell me where ... is?	**Kunt u mij zeggen waar ... is?**	kurnt ew maiy **zeh**ghern Ꝟaar ... iss
Where can I find this address?	**Waar is dit adres?**	Ꝟaar iss dit aa**drehss**
Where's this?	**Waar is dat?**	Ꝟaar iss daht

Miles into kilometres										
1 mile = 1.609 kilometres (km)										
miles	10	20	30	40	50	60	70	80	90	100
km	16	32	48	64	80	97	113	129	145	161

Kilometres into miles													
1 kilometre (km) = 0.62 miles													
km	10	20	30	40	50	60	70	80	90	100	110	120	130
miles	6	12	19	25	31	37	44	50	56	62	68	75	81

Can you show me on the map where I am?	**Kunt u mij op de kaart aanwijzen waar ik ben?**	kurnt ew maiy op der kaart **aan**√aiyzern √aar ik behn
Can you show me on the map where the university is?	**Kunt u mij op de kaart aanwijzen waar de universiteit is?**	kurnt ew maiy op der kaart **aan**√aiyzern √aar der ewneevehrsee**taiyt** iss
Can I park there?	**Kan ik daar parkeren?**	kahn ik daar pahr**kay**rern
Is that a one-way street?	**Is dat een straat met eenrichtingsver-keer?**	iss daht ayn straat meht ayn**rikh**tingsverr**kayr**
Does the traffic got this way?	**Is het verkeer in deze richting?**	iss heht verr**kayr** in **dayzer** **rikh**ting

U zit op de verkeerde weg.	You're on the wrong road.
U moet rechtdoor rijden.	Go straight ahead.
Het is verderop...	It's down there on the...
rechts/links	right/left
Volg deze weg tot het eerste/tweede kruispunt.	Go to the first/second crossroads.
Sla bij de stoplichten links af.	Turn to the left at the traffic lights.
Sla rechtsaf bij de volgende hoek.	Turn right at the next corner.

In the rest of this section we'll be more closely concerned with the car itself. We've divided it into two parts:

Part A contains general advice on motoring in Holland and Belgium. It's essentially for reference and is therefore to be browsed over, preferably in advance.

Part B is concerned with the practical details of accidents and breakdown. It includes a list of car parts and of things that may go wrong with them. All you have to do is to show it to the garage mechanic and get him to point to the items required.

Part A

Customs—Documentation

You will need the following documents when driving in Holland and Belgium:

- passport
- international insurance certificate (green card)
- car registration papers (log book)
- valid driving licence

Motor vehicles must carry a nationality plate or sticker. In Holland you can drive with a British or American driving licence. However, if you intend to travel through other countries, an international driving licence may prove a useful document to have. Cars may be kept in the country without special permission for a period not exceeding a year. No frontier documents are required for trailers and caravans, except for a valid registration certificate.

Here's my...	**Hier is mijn...**	heer iss maiyn
driving licence	**rijbewijs**	raiyberʋaiyss
green card	**groene kaart**	ghrooner kaart
passport	**paspoort**	pahspoart
registration (log) book	**kentekenbewijs**	kehntaykernberʋaiyss
We're staying for...	**Wij blijven...**	ʋaiy **blaiy**vern
three days	**3 dagen**	3 **daa**ghern
a week	**een week**	ayn ʋayk
two weeks	**2 weken**	2 **ʋay**kern
a month	**een maand**	ayn maant
I've nothing to declare.	**Ik heb niets aan te geven.**	ik hehp neets aan ter **ghay**vern

A red warning triangle—for display on the road in case of breakdown or accident—is compulsory; parking lights are advisable. Crash helmets are compulsory for both riders and passengers on motorcycles and scooters. If a foreign visitor's car is fitted with seat belts, they must be worn.

Driving

In Holland, roads are classified as follows:

A. 6	*Autoweg* (**oa**toa√ehkh)—a motorway or expressway. A toll is not usually levied for motorways, but it does exist for bridges and tunnels.
E 2	European motorway. A green sign with white lettering.
N 10	National road. Usually only one traffic lane in each direction.
B-weg	Secondary road.

Roads are generally good in Holland and Belgium. Foreign drivers should take special care until they are familiar with the driving habits of the country. In Holland and Belgium you drive on the right and overtake (pass) on the left. When overtaking, you must use your indicator. Adapt your speed to road and traffic conditions, and don't get hot under the collar if local drivers seem impatient.

Pedestrians on zebra crossings (indicated by black and white stripes on the road) must be given unimpeded passage. Trams have priority over other traffic (police, ambulance and fire engines excepted). Watch out for passengers alighting at tramstops.

Unless otherwise indicated, traffic coming from the right has priority over traffic going straight on. An orange-coloured, diamond-shaped sign with a white border indicates you have the right of way. Fast-moving traffic has priority over slow-moving traffic (cyclists, mopeds, cart-drivers etc.). Cyclists require special attention in Holland. They abound!

Within cities and other populated areas the speed limit is 50 kilometres per hour (kph)—31 mph—with the exception of posted areas permitting 80 kph (44 mph). Outside built-up areas and on motorways the speed limit is 100 kph (62 mph). For cars with trailers or caravans the speed limit is 80 kph on all roads.

The police are normally quite lenient with tourists, but don't push your luck too far. For small offences you can be fined on the spot. Here are some phrases which may come in handy, but if you're in serious trouble, insist on having an interpreter.

I'm sorry, Officer, I didn't see the sign.	**Neemt u mij niet kwalijk, agent, ik heb het verkeersbord niet gezien.**	naymt ew maiy neet k**ʋaa**lerk aa**ghehnt** ik hehp heht verr**kayrs**bort neet gher**zeen**
The light was green.	**Het verkeerslicht was groen.**	heht verr**kayrs**likht ʋahss ghroon
I don't understand.	**Ik begrijp het niet.**	ik ber**ghraiyp** heht neet
How much is the fine?	**Hoeveel is de boete?**	hoo**vayl** iss der **boo**ter

Parking

As at home, parking is a headache in most cities, particularly in metropolitan areas or popular holiday resorts. Most cities have introduced parking meters and "blue zones" for which parking discs are compulsory.

Excuse me. May I park here?	**Neemt u mij niet kwalijk, mag ik hier parkeren?**	naymt ew maiy neet k**ʋaa**lerk mahkh ik heer pahr**kay**rern
How long can I park here?	**Hoe lang mag ik hier blijven staan?**	hoo lahng mahkh ik heer **blaiy**vern staan
Excuse me. Do you have some change for the parking meter?	**Neemt u mij niet kwalijk. Hebt u wat kleingeld voor de parkeermeter?**	naymt ew maiy neet k**ʋaa**lerk hehpt ew ʋaht klaiyn**ghehlt** voar der pahr**kayr**mayterr

Road signs

Road signs are practically standardized throughout Western Europe and are quickly learnt. The main ones are shown on pages 160 and 161.

Listed below are some written signs which you'll certainly encounter when driving in Holland and Belgium.

ALLEEN VOOR VOETGANGERS	Pedestrians only
BEPERKTE DOORRIJ-HOOGTE	Height limit
BUSHALTE	Bus stop
DOORGAAND VERKEER	Through traffic
DOORGAAND VERKEER GESTREMD	No through road
EENRICHTINGSVERKEER	One way traffic
EINDE INHAALVERBOD	End of no-pass zone
FIETSERS	(Watch out for) cyclists
FILEVORMING	Bottleneck
GEVAAR	Danger
GEVAARLIJKE BOCHT	Dangerous bend (curve)
INHAALVERBOD	No overtaking (passing)
INRIJDEN VERBODEN	No entry
LANGZAAM RIJDEN	Reduce speed
LOSSE STEENSLAG	Loose gravel
OMLEIDING	Diversion (detour)
PARKEERVERBOD	No parking
RECHTS HOUDEN	Keep right
SLECHT WEGDEK	Bad road surface
STOPLICHTEN OP 100 M	Traffic lights at 100 metres
TEGENLIGGERS	Oncoming traffic
VERKEER OVER EEN RIJBAAN	Traffic in single lane
VOETGANGERS	(Watch out for) pedestrians
WACHTVERBOD	No waiting
WEGOMLEGGING	Diversion (detour)
WERK IN UITVOERING	Roadworks (men working)
WIELRIJDERS	Cyclists
ZACHTE BERM	Soft shoulders

Part B

Accidents

This section is confined to immediate aid. The legal problems of responsibility and settlement can be taken care of later. Your first concern will be for the injured.

Is anyone hurt?	**Is er iemand gewond?**	iss ehr **ee**mahnt gher**ʋont**
Don't move.	**Beweeg u niet.**	ber**ʋaykh** ew neet
It's all right.	**Het is niet erg.**	heht iss neet ehrkh
Don't worry.	**Maakt u zich geen zorgen.**	maakt ew zikh ghayn **zor**ghern
Where's the nearest telephone?	**Waar is de dichtstbijzijnde telefoon?**	ʋaar iss der dikhtst-baiy**zaiy**nder tayler**foan**
Can I use your telephone? There's been an accident.	**Mag ik van uw telefoon gebruik maken? Er is een ongeluk gebeurd.**	mahkh ik vahn ew^{ee} tayler**foan** gher**brur^{ew}k** **maa**kern? ehr iss ayn **on**gherlurk gher**burrt**
Call a doctor/an ambulance quickly.	**Waarschuw onmiddelijk een doktor/ziekenauto.**	**ʋaar**skhew^{ee} on**mid**derlerk ayn **dok**terr/**zee**kerno^{ow}toa
There are people injured.	**Er zijn gewonden.**	ehr zaiyn gher**ʋon**dern
Help me get them out of the car.	**Helpt u mij ze uit de auto te halen.**	hehlpt ew maiy zer ur^{ew}t der o^{ow}toa ter **haa**lern

Police—Exchange of information

Please call the police.	**Waarschuw de politie, alstublieft.**	**ʋaar**skhew^{ee} der poa**leet**see ahlstew**bleeft**
There's been an accident. It's about 2 km from...	**Er is een ongeluk gebeurd. Het is ongeveer 2 km van ...**	eht iss ayn **on**gherlurk gher**burrt**. heht iss **on**ghervayr 2 **kee**loamayterr vahn
I'm on the Amsterdam-Utrecht road, 10 km from Amsterdam.	**Ik ben op de weg Amsterdam-Utrecht, 10 km van Amsterdam.**	ik behn op der ʋehkh ahmsterr**dahm**-**ew**trehkht 10 **kee**loamayterr vahn ahmsterr**dahm**

FOR DOCTOR, see page 162

Here's my name and address.	**Hier is mijn naam en adres.**	heer iss maiyn naam ehn **aa**drehss
Would you mind acting as a witness?	**Wilt u als getuige optreden?**	ꝟilt ew ahls gher**tur^{ew}**gher **op**traydern
I'd like an interpreter.	**Ik wil graag een tolk.**	ik ꝟil ghraakh ayn tolk

Remember to put out a red warning triangle if the car is out of action or impeding traffic.

B-r-e-a-k-d-o-w-n

...and that's what we'll do with this section: break it down into four phases.

1. **On the road**
   You ask where the nearest garage is.
2. **At the garage**
   You tell the mechanic what's wrong.
3. **Finding the trouble**
   He tells you what he thinks is wrong.
4. **Getting it repaired**
   You tell him to repair it and, once that's over, settle the account (or argue about it).

Phase 1—On the road

Where's the nearest garage?	**Waar is de dichtstbijzijnde garage?**	ꝟaar iss der dikhtst-baiy**zaiyn**der ghaa**raa**zher
Excuse me. My car has broken down. May I use your phone?	**Neemt u mij niet kwalijk. Ik heb autopech. Mag ik even opbellen?**	naymt ew maiy neet kꝟ**aa**lerk. ik hehp o^{ow}toapehkh. mahkh ik ayvern **op**behlern
What's the telephone number of the nearest garage?	**Wat is het telefoonnummer van de dichtstbijzijnde garage?**	ꝟaht iss heht taylerf**oan**-nurmerr vahn der dikhtst-baiy**zaiyn**der ghaa**raa**zher
I've had a breakdown at...	**Ik sta met motorpech in...**	ik staa meht **moa**terrpehkh in

Can you send a mechanic?	**Kunt u een monteur sturen?**	kurnt ew ayn mon**turr** **stew**rern
Can you send a truck to tow my car?	**Kunt u een takelwagen sturen?**	kurnt ew ayn **taa**kerl-Vaaghern **stew**rern
How long will you be?	**Hoe lang duurt het voordat U komt?**	hoo lahng dewrt heht voardaht ew komt

Phase 2—At the garage

Can you help me?	**Kunt u mij helpen?**	kurnt ew maiy **hehl**pern
I think there's something wrong with the...	**Ik denk dat er iets mis is met...**	ik dehnk daht ehr eets mis iss meht
battery	**de batterij**	der bahtter**raiy**
brakes	**de remmen**	der **reh**mern
bulbs	**de lampen**	der **lahm**pern
carburettor	**de carburator**	der kahrbew**raa**tor
clutch	**de koppeling**	der **kop**perling
cooling system	**het koelsysteem**	heht **kool**seestaym
contact	**het contact**	heht kon**tahkt**
dipswitch (dimmer switch)	**de dimschakelaar**	der **dim**skhaakerlaar
dynamo	**de dynamo**	der **dee**naamoa
electrical system	**het elektrisch circuit**	heht ay**lehk**treess sirk**Veet**
engine	**de motor**	der **moa**terr
exhaust pipe	**de uitlaatpijp**	der **ur^{ew}**tlaatpaiyp
fan	**de ventilator**	der vehntee**laa**tor
filter	**de oliefilter**	der **oa**leefilterr
fuel pump	**de benzinepomp**	der behn**zee**nerpomp
fuel tank	**de benzinetank**	der behn**zee**nertehnk
gears	**de versnelling**	der verr**sneh**ling
generator	**de dynamo**	der **dee**naamoa
hand brake	**de handremmen**	der **hahnt**rehmern
headlights	**de koplampen**	der **kop**lahmpern
heating	**de verwarming**	der verr**Vahr**ming
horn	**de claxon**	der **klahk**son
ignition system	**de ontsteking**	der ont**stay**king
indicator	**de richtingaanwijzer**	der rikhtingaan**Vaiy**zerr
lights	**de lichten**	der **likh**tern
back-up lights	**de achteruitrijlichten**	der ahkhterr**ur^{ew}**traiy-likhtern
brake lights	**de remlichten**	der **rehm**likhtern

rear lights	**de achterlichten**	der **ahkh**terrlikhtern
reversing lights	**de achteruitrij-lichten**	der ahkhterr**ur**^{ew}traiy-likhtern
tail lights	**de achterlichten**	der **ahkh**terrlikhtern
lining and covering	**de remvoering**	der **rehm**vooring
lubrication system	**de oliedruk**	der **oa**leedrurk
muffler	**de knaldemper**	der **knahl**dehmperr
parking brake	**de handrem**	der **hahnt**rehm
radiator	**de radiator**	der raadee**yaa**tor
reflectors	**de reflectoren**	der rayflehk**toa**rern
seat	**de zitting**	der **zit**ting
silencer	**de knalpot**	der **knahl**pot
sliding roof	**het open dak**	heht **oa**pern dahk
sparking plugs	**de bougies**	der boo**zhee**ss
speedometer	**de snelheidsmeter**	der **snehl**haiytsmayterr
starter	**de starter**	der **stahr**terr
steering	**de stuurinrichting**	der **stewr**intikhting
suspension	**de vering**	der **vay**ring
transmission	**de versnelling**	der verr**sneh**ling
automatic transmission	**de automatische versnelling**	der oato**maa**teesser verr**sneh**ling
turn signal	**de richtingaanwijzer**	der rikhtingaanVaiyzerr
wheels	**de wielen**	der **Vee**lern
wipers	**de ruitenwissers**	der **rur**^{ew}terVisserrss

LEFT	RIGHT
LINKS	**RECHTS**
(links)	(rehkhts)

FRONT	BACK
VOORKANT	**ACHTERKANT**
(voar)	(ahkhterr)

It's…	**Het…**	heht
bad	**loopt slecht**	loapt slehkht
blowing	**brandt door**	brahnt doar
blown	**is doorgeslagen**	iss **doar**gherslaaghern
broken	**is gebroken**	iss gher**broa**kern
burnt	**is doorgebrand**	iss **doar**gherbrahnt
cracked	**is gebarsten**	iss gher**bah**stern
defective	**is kapot**	iss kaa**pot**
disconnected	**is losgeraakt**	iss **los**gherraakt
dry	**is droog gelopen**	iss droakh ghe**hloa**pern
frozen	**is bevroren**	iss berr**vroa**rern
jammed	**is geblokkeerd**	iss gherblok**kayrt**
knocking	**rammelt**	**rah**merlt
leaking	**lekt**	lehkt

loose	**heeft losgelaten**	hayft loasghehl**aa**tern
misfiring	**slaat over**	slaat **oa**verr
noisy	**maakt lawaai**	maakt laa**√aa**^{ee}
not working	**doet het niet**	doot heht neet
overheating	**loopt warm**	loapt √ahrm
short-circuiting	**maakt kortsluiting**	maakt **korts**lur^{ew}ting
slack	**is slap**	iss slahp
slipping	**slipt**	slipt
stuck	**zit vast**	zit vahst
vibrating	**trilt**	trilt
weak	**is bezweken**	iss behz**√eh**kehrn
worn	**is versleten**	iss verr**slay**tern
The car won't start.	**De auto wil niet starten.**	der **o**^{ow}toa √il neet **stahr**tern
It's locked and the keys are inside.	**Hij zit op slot en de sleutels zitten erin.**	haiy zit op slot ehn der **slur**terlss zittern ehrin
The fan belt is too slack.	**De ventilatorriem is te slap.**	der vehntee**laa**torreem iss ter slahp
The radiator is leaking.	**De radiator lekt.**	der raadeeyaator lehkt
The idling needs adjusting.	**De stationair moet bijgesteld worden.**	der staasyoa**nehr** moot **baiy**gherstehlt √ordern
The clutch engages too quickly.	**De koppeling pakt te snel.**	der **kop**perling pahkt ter snehl
The steering wheel is vibrating.	**Het stuur trilt.**	heht stewr trilt
The wipers are smearing.	**De ruitewissers maken de ruit niet schoon.**	der **rur**^{ew}tereisserr **maa**kern der rur^{ew}t neet skhoan
The pneumatic suspension is weak.	**De luchtvering is slap.**	der **lurkht**vayring iss slahp

Now that you've explained what's wrong, you'll want to know how long it'll take to repair it and make your arrangements accordingly.

How long will it take to repair?	**Hoe lang duurt de reparatie?**	how lahng dewrt der raypaa**raat**see
How long will it take to find out what's wrong?	**Wanneer weet u wat er aan mankeert?**	√ahnayr √ayt ew √aht ehr aan mahn**kayrt**

Suppose I come back in half an hour?	**Zal ik over een half uur terugkomen?**	zahl ik **oa**verr ayn hahlf ewr terr**urkh**koamern
Can you give me a lift into town?	**Kunt u mij een lift naar de stad geven?**	kurnt ew maiy ayn lift naar der staht **ghay**vern

Phase 3—Finding the trouble

It's up to the mechanic to find the trouble and to repair it if possible. All you have to do is hand him the book and point to the text in Dutch below.

Wilt u a.u.b. op deze alfabetische lijst aanwijzen welk onderdeel defect is. Als uw klant wil weten wat eraan mankeert, wijs hem dan in de volgende lijst de term aan die hierop van toepassing is (gebroken, kortsluiting, enz.).*

accu	battery
accucellen	battery cells
accuvloeistof	battery liquid
anker van de magneet	starter armature
as	shaft
automatische transmissie (overbrenging)	automatic transmission
batterij	battery
benzinefilter	petrol (gas) filter
benzinepomp	petrol (gas) pump
bougies	sparking plugs
carburator	carburettor
cardankoppeling	universal joint
carter	crankcase
cilinder	cylinder
cilinderhoofd	cylinder head
cilinderkoppakking	cylinder head gasket
condensator	condensor
contact	contact
contactpunten	points
dimschakelaar	dipswitch (dimmer switch)

* Please look at the following alphabetical list and point to the defective item. If your customer wants to know what's wrong with it, pick the applicable term from the next list (broken, short-circuited, etc.).

drukveren	pressure springs
electrisch circuit	electrical system
filter	filter
gedistilleerd water	distilled water
hoofdlagers	main bearings
injectiepomp	injection pump
koelsysteem	cooling system
kabel	cable
kabels van de bougies	sparking-plug leads
kabels van de verdeler	distributor leads
klepstoters	tappets
koolborstels	brushes
koppeling	clutch
koppelingspedaal	clutch pedal
koppelingsplaat	clutch plate
krukas	crankshaft
lagers	bearings
luchtfilter	air filter
luchtvering	pneumatic suspension
membraan	diaphragm
motor	motor
motorblok	block
nokkenas	camshaft
oliefilter	oil filter
oliepomp	oil pump
ontsteking	ignition coil
ophanging	suspension
overbrenging	transmission
pomp	pump
radiator	radiator
remblokken	brake shoes
remmen	brakes
remtrommel	brake drum
remvoering	brake lining
ringen	rings
schokbrekers	shock absorber
smeervet	grease
spoorstangeinden	track-rod ends
stabilisator	stabilizer
stangen	stems
startmotor	starter motor
stuurblok	steering column
stuurinrichting	steering
stuurhuis	steering box
stuurstang	steering post
tandheugel en tandwiel	rack and pinion

tandwielen	teeth
thermostaat	thermostat
transmissie	transmission
transmissie-as	prop shaft
ventiel	valve
ventielveer	valve spring
ventilator	fan
ventilatorriem	fan belt
verbinding	connection
verdeler	distributor
veren	springs
vering	suspension
versnelling	gear
versnellingsbak	gearbox
vlotter	float
waterpomp	water pump
wielen	wheels
zuiger	piston
zuigerringen	piston rings

De volgende lijst bevat woorden die beschrijven wat eraan de auto mankeert of wat eraan gedaan moet worden.*

aandraaien	to tighten
bevroren	frozen
bijstellen	to adjust
bijvijlen	to grind in
defekt	defective
doorgeslagen	blown
droog	dry
gebarsten	cracked
geblokkeerd	jammed
gebroken	broken
heeft speling	loose
hoog	high
kort	short
laag	low
lek	punctured/blown
lekt	leaking
los	disconnected
losser maken	to loosen

* The following list contains words which describe what's wrong as well as what may need to be done.

maakt kortsluiting	short-circuited
ontluchten	to bleed
opladen	to charge
opnieuw voeren	to reline
oververhitting	overheating
schoonmaken	to clean
slaat over	misfiring
slap	slack
slipt	slipping
snel	quick
speling	play
stoot	knocking
trilt	vibrating
uitbalanceren	to balance
uit elkaar halen	to strip down
vastgelopen	stuck
veranderen	to change
verbogen	warped
verbrand	burnt
verroest	rusty
versleten	worn
vervangen	to replace
vibreert	vibrating
vuil	dirty
zwak	weak

Phase 4—Getting it repaired

Have you found the trouble?	**Hebt u het defect gevonden?**	hehpt ew heht der**fehkt** ghervondern

Now that you know what's wrong, or at least have some idea, you'll want to find out…

Is that serious?	**Is het ernstig?**	iss heht **ehrn**sterkh
Can you repair it?	**Kunt u het repareren?**	kurnt ew heht raypaarayrern
Can you do it now?	**Kunt u het meteen doen?**	kurnt ew heht mer**tayn** doon
What's it going to cost?	**Hoeveel gaat het kosten?**	hoo**vayl** ghaat heht **kos**tern
Do you have the necessary spare parts?	**Hebt u de nodige onderdelen in reserve?**	hehpt ew der **noa**dergher onderrdaylern in rer**sehr**ver

What if he says "no"?

Why can't you do it?	**Waarom kunt u het niet doen?**	√**aarom** kurnt ew heht neet doon
Is it essential to have that part?	**Is dat onderdeel absoluut noodzakelijk?**	iss daht **on**derrdayl ahpsoa**lewt** noat**zaa**kerlerk
How long is it going to take to get the spare parts?	**Hoe lang duurt het voordat u die onderdelen hebt?**	hoo lahng dewrt heht **voar**daht ew dee **on**derrdaylern hehpt
Where's the nearest garage that can repair it?	**Waar is de dichtstbijzijnde garage waar dit wel gerepareerd kan worden?**	√aar iss der dikhtst-baiy**zaiyn**der ghaa**raa**zher √aar dit √ehl gherray-paa**rayrt** kahn √**or**dern
Can you fix it so that I can get as far as...?	**Kunt u het zo repareren dat ik naar ... kan rijden?**	kurnt ew heht zoa raypaa**ray**rern daht ik naar ... kahn **raiy**dern

Setting the bill

If you're really stuck, ask if you can leave the car at the garage. Contact the automobile association or hire another car.

Is everything fixed?	**Is het weer helemaal in orde?**	iss heht √ayr **hay**lermaal in **or**der
How much do I owe you?	**Hoeveel ben ik u schuldig?**	hoo**vayl** behn ik ew **skhurl**derkh
This is for you.	**Dit is voor u.**	dit iss voar ew

But you may feel that the workmanship is sloppy or that you're paying for work not done. Get the bill itemized. If necessary, get it translated before you pay.

I'd like to check the bill first. Will you itemize the work done?	**Ik wil graag eerst de rekening controleren. Wilt u al het verrichte werk in de rekening specificeren?**	ik √il ghraakh ayrst der **ray**kerning kontroa**lay**rern. √ilt ew ahl heht ver**rikh**ter √ehrk in der **ray**kerning spayseefee**say**rern

If the garage still won't back down and you're sure you're right, get the help of a third party.

Some international road signs

No vehicles

No entry

No overtaking (passing)

Oncoming traffic has priority

Maximum speed limit

No parking

Caution

Intersection

Dangerous bend (curve)

Road narrows

Intersection with secondary road

Two-way traffic

Dangerous hill

Uneven road

Falling rocks

Give way (yield)

Main road, thoroughfare

End of restriction

One-way traffic

Traffic goes this way

Roundabout (rotary)

Bicycles only

Pedestrians only

Minimum speed limit

Keep right (left if symbol reversed)

Parking

Hospital

Motorway (expressway)

Motor vehicles only

Filling station

No through road

Doctor

Frankly, how much use is a phrase book going to be to you in case of serious injury or illness? The only phrase you need in such an emergency is:

Get a doctor quickly!	**Haal vlug een dokter!**	haal vlurkh ayn **dok**terr

But there are minor aches and pains, ailments and irritations that can upset the best planned trip. Here we can help you and, perhaps, the doctor.

Some doctors will speak English well; others will know enough for your needs. But suppose there's something the doctor can't explain because of language difficulties? We've thought of that. As you'll see, this section has been arranged to enable you and the doctor to communicate. From pages 165 to 171, you'll find your part of the dialogue on the upper half of each page—the doctor's part is on the lower half.

The whole section has been divided into three parts: illness, wounds, nervous tension. Page 171 is concerned with prescriptions and fees.

General

Can you get me a doctor?	**Kunt u een dokter roepen?**	kurnt ew ayn **dok**terr **roo**pern
Is there a doctor here?	**Is er hier een dokter?**	iss ehr heer ayn **dok**terr
Please telephone for a doctor immediately.	**Telefoneer zo vlug mogelijk een dokter, alstublieft.**	taylerfoa**nayr** zoa vlurkh **moa**gherlerk ayn **dok**terr ahlstew**bleeft**
Where's there a doctor who speaks English?	**Waar kan ik een dokter vinden die Engels spreekt?**	ѵaar kahn ik ayn **dok**terr **vin**dern dee **ehn**gerlss spraykt
Where's the surgery (doctor's office)?	**Waar heeft de dokter zijn praktijk?**	ѵaar hayft der **dok**terr zaiyn prahk**taiyk**

FOR PHARMACY, see page 108

DOCTOR

What are the surgery (office) hours?	**Hoe laat is het spreekuur?**	hoo laat iss heht **spray**kewr
Could the doctor come and see me here?	**Zou de dokter mij hier kunnen bezoeken?**	zo^ow der **dok**terr maiy heer **kur**nern ber**zoo**kern
What time can the doctor come?	**Hoe laat kan de dokter komen?**	hoo laat kahn der **dok**terr **koa**mern

Symptoms

Use this section to tell the doctor what's wrong. Basically, what he'll require to know is:

What? (ache, pain, bruise, etc.)
Where? (arm, stomach, etc.)
How long? (have you had the trouble)

Before you visit the doctor find out the answers to these questions by glancing through the pages that follow. In this way you'll save time.

Parts of the body

ankle	**de enkel**	der **ehn**kerl
appendix	**de blindedarm**	der **blin**derdahrm
arm	**de arm**	der ahrm
artery	**de slagader**	der **slahgh**aaderr
back	**de rug**	der rurkh
bladder	**de blaas**	der blaass
blood	**het bloed**	heht bloot
bone	**het bot**	heht bot
bowels	**de darmen**	der **dahr**mern
breast	**de borstkas**	der borst
cheek	**de wang**	der ∀ahng
chest	**de borst**	der borst
chin	**de kin**	der kin
collar-bone	**het sleutelbeen**	heht **slur**terlbayn
ear	**het oor**	heht oar
elbow	**de elleboog**	der **eh**lerboakh
eye	**het oog**	heht oakh
face	**het gezicht**	heht gher**zikht**
finger	**de vinger**	der **ving**err
foot	**de voet**	der voot
forehead	**het voorhoofd**	heht **voar**hoaft

gland	**de klier**	der kleer
hair	**het haar**	heht haar
hand	**de hand**	der hahnt
head	**het hoofd**	heht hoaft
heart	**het hart**	heht hahrt
heel	**de hiel**	der heel
hip	**de heup**	der hurp
intestines	**de ingewanden**	der ingherVahndern
jaw	**de kaak**	der kaak
joint	**het gewricht**	heht gherVrikht
kidney	**de nier**	der neer
knee	**de knie**	der knee
knee cap	**de knieschijf**	der kneeskhaiyf
leg	**het been**	heht bayn
lip	**de lip**	der lip
liver	**de lever**	der layverr
lung	**de long**	der long
mouth	**de mond**	der mont
muscle	**de spier**	der speer
neck	**de nek**	der nehk
nerve	**de zenuw**	der zaynew^{oo}
nervous system	**het zenuwstelsel**	heht zaynew^{oo}stehlserl
nose	**de neus**	der nurss
rib	**de rib**	der rip
shoulder	**de schouder**	der skho^{ow}derr
skin	**de huid**	der hur^{ew}t
spine	**de ruggegraat**	der rurgherghraat
stomach	**de maag**	der maakh
tendon	**de pees**	der payss
thigh	**de dij**	der daiy
throat	**de keel**	der kayl
thumb	**de duim**	der dur^{ew}m
toe	**de teen**	der tayn
tongue	**de tong**	der ting
tonsils	**de amandelen**	der aamahnderlern
urine	**de urine**	der ewreener
vein	**de ader**	der aaderr
wrist	**de pols**	der polss

LEFT/ON THE LEFT SIDE

LINKS/AAN DE LINKERKANT

(links/aan der linkerrkahnt)

RIGHT/ON THE RIGHT SIDE

RECHTS/AAN DE RECHTERKANT

(rehkhts/aan der rehkhterrkahnt)

PATIENT

Part 1—Illness

I'm not feeling well.	**Ik voel mij niet goed.**	ik vool maiy neet ghoot
I'm ill.	**Ik ben ziek.**	ik behn zeek
I've got a pain here.	**Ik heb hier pijn.**	ik hehp heer paiyn
His/Her ... hurts.	**Zijn/Haar ... doet pijn.**	zaiyn/haar ... doot paiyn
I've got a...	**Ik heb...**	ik hehp
backache/ fever/ headache/ sore throat	**hoofdpijn/rugpijn koorts/keelpijn**	**hoaft**paiyn/**rurgh**paiyn koarts/**kayl**paiyn
I suffer from travel sickness.	**Ik ben wagenziek.**	ik behn Vaaghernzeek
I'm constipated.	**Ik heb last van constipatie**	ik hehp lahst vahn konsteepaatsee
I've been vomiting.	**Ik heb overgegeven.**	ik hehp oaverrgherghayvern

---

DOCTOR

1—Ziekte

Wat is er aan de hand?	What's the trouble?
Waar doet het pijn?	Where does it hurt?
Hoe lang hebt u die pijn al?	How long have you had this pain?
Wat voor een soort pijn voelt u?	What sort of pain is it?
dof/hevig/bonzend voortdurend/af en toe	dull/sharp/throbbing constant/on and off
Hoe lang voelt u zich al zo?	How long have you been feeling like this?
Stroop uw mouw op, alstublieft.	Roll up your sleeve.
Kleedt u zich uit (tot het middel), alstublieft.	Please undress (to the waist).

PATIENT

I feel faint.	**Ik voel mij slap.**	ik vool maiy slahp
I feel…	**Ik ben…**	ik behn
dizzy	**duizelig**	**dur^{ew}**zerlerkh
nauseous	**misselijk**	**miss**erlerk
shivery	**rillerig**	**rill**errerkh
I've/He's/She's got a/an…	**Ik heb/Hij heeft/ Zij heeft…**	ik hehp/haiy hayft/ zaiy hayft
abscess	**een abces**	ayn ahp**sehss**
asthma	**asthma**	**ahst**maa
boil	**een steenpuist**	ayn **staynpur^{ew}st**
chill	**kou gevat**	**ko^{ow}** ghervaht
cold	**een verkoudheid**	ayn verr**ko^{ow}t**haiyt
convulsions	**stuiptrekkingen**	**stur^{ew}p**trehkkingern
cramps	**krampen**	**krahm**pern
diarrhoea	**diarrhee**	deeyaa**ray**
fever	**koorts**	koarts
haemorrhoids	**aambeien**	**aam**baiyyern
hay fever	**hooikoorts**	**hoa^{ee}**koarts
hernia	**een hernia**	ayn **hehr**neeyaa
indigestion	**een indigestie**	ayn indee**ghehs**tee

DOCTOR

Gaat u hier liggen, a.u.b.	Please lie down over here.
Open uw mond, alstublieft.	Open your mouth.
Diep inademen.	Breathe deeply.
Hoest u eens, alstublieft.	Cough, please.
Ik zal uw temperatuur opnemen.	I'll take your temperature.
Ik zal uw bloeddruk opmeten.	I'm going to take your blood pressure.
Is dit de eerste keer dat u hier last van hebt?	Is this the first time you've had this?
Ik zal u een injectie geven.	I'll give you an injection.
Ik wil een flesje urine/ontlasting van u hebben.	I want a specimen of your urine/stools.

PATIENT

inflammation of ...	**een ontsteking aan ...**	ayn ont**stay**king aan
influenza	**griep**	ghreep
morning sickness	**last van misselijkheid**	lahst vahn **mis**serlerkhaiyt
a rash	**uitslag**	**ur^{ew}t**slahkh
rheumatism	**reumatiek**	rurmaa**teek**
palpitations	**hartkloppingen**	**hahrt**klopingern
stiff neck	**een stijve nek**	ayn **stai**yver nehk
sunburn	**zonnebrand**	**zon**nerbrahnt
sunstroke	**een zonnesteek**	ayn **zon**nerstayk
tonsilitis	**een amandelonsteking**	ayn aa**mahn**derlontstayking
ulcer	**een zweer**	ayn zʋayr
It's nothing serious, I hope?	**Het is toch niets ernstigs, hoop ik?**	heht iss tokh neets **ehrn**sterghss hoap ik
Is it contagious?	**Is het besmettelijk?**	iss heht ber**smeh**terlerk
I'd like you to prescribe some medicine for me.	**Ik zou graag een recept van u willen hebben.**	ik zo^{ow} ghraakh ayn rer**sehpt** vahn ew **ʋ**illern **heh**bern

---

DOCTOR

Het is niets ernstigs.	It's nothing to worry about.
U moet ... dagen in bed blijven.	You must stay in bed for ... days.
U hebt ...	You've got ...
een blindedarmontsteking	appendicitis
een gewrichtsontsteking	arthritis
een darmgriep	gastric flu
voedselvergiftiging	food poisoning
een blaasontsteking	cystitis
een oorontsteking	otitis
een longontsteking	pneumonia
voorhoofdholte-onsteking	sinusitis
een keelontsteking	throat infection
Ik stuur u naar het ziekenhuis voor een algemeen onderzoek.	I want you to go to the hospital for a general check-up.
Ik stuur u naar een specialist door.	I want you to see a specialist.

PATIENT

I'm diabetic.	**Ik ben suiker-patiënt.**	ik behn **sur^{ew}kerrpaasyehnt**
I've a cardiac condition.	**Ik ben hart-patiënt.**	ik behn **hahrt**paasyehnt
I had a heart attack in…	**Ik heb in … een hartaanval gehad.**	ik hehp in … ayn **hahrt-aanvahl** gher**haht**
I'm allergic to…	**Ik ben allergisch voor…**	ik behn **aallehrgheess** voar
This is my usual medicine.	**Dit medicijn gebruik ik gewoonlijk.**	dit maydee**saiyn** gher-**brur^{ew}k** ik gher**V**oanlerk
I need this medicine.	**Ik heb deze medicijn nodig.**	ik hehp **dayzer** maydee-**saiyn noa**derkh
I'm expecting a baby.	**Ik verwacht een baby.**	ik verr**Vahkht** ayn **baybee**
Can I travel?	**Mag ik reizen?**	mahkh ik **raiy**zern

DOCTOR

Hoeveel insuline gebruikt u?	What dose of insulin are you taking?
Injecties of medicijnen?	Injection or oral?
Wat voor behandeling hebt u gehad?	What treatment have you been having?
Welke medicijnen neemt u in?	What medicine have you been taking?
U hebt een (lichte) hartaanval gehad.	You've had a (slight) heart attack.
… wordt niet in Nederland/ België gebruikt. Dit is ongeveer hetzelfde.	We don't use … in Holland/Belgium. This is very similar.
Wanneer verwacht u de baby?	When's the baby due?
U mag tot … niet reizen.	You can't travel until…

PATIENT

Part 2—Wounds

I've got a/an… Could you have a look at it?	**Ik heb … Kunt u het even onderzoeken?**	ik hehp … kurnt ew heht **ay**vern onder**zoo**kern
blister	**een blaar**	ayn blaar
boil	**een steenpuist**	ayn **stayn**pur^{ew}st
bruise	**een kneuzing**	ayn **knur**zing
burn	**een brandwond**	ayn **brahnt**ʋont
cut	**een snijwond**	ayn **snaiy**ʋont
graze	**een schaafwond**	ayn **skhaaf**ʋont
insect bite	**een insektenbeet**	ayn in**sehk**ternbayt
lump	**een bult**	ayn burlt
rash	**uitslag**	**ur^{ew}t**slahkh
sting	**een steek**	ayn stayk
swelling	**een zwelling**	ayn **zʋeh**ling
wound	**een wond**	ayn ʋont
I can't move my … It hurts.	**Ik kan mijn … niet bewegen. Het doet pijn.**	ik kahn maiyn … neet ber**ʋay**ghern. heht doot paiyn

---

DOCTOR

2—Verwondingen

Het is (niet) ontstoken.	It's (not) infected.
U hebt een hernia.	You've got a slipped disc.
Er moet een röntgenfoto gemaakt worden.	I want you to have an X-ray taken.
Het is…	It's…
gebroken/verstuikt ontwricht/gescheurd	broken/sprained dislocated/torn
U hebt een spier verrekt.	You've pulled a muscle.
Ik zal u een antiseptisch middel geven. Het is niet ernstig.	I'll give you an antiseptic. It's not serious.
Bent u tegen tetanus ingeënt?	Have you been vaccinated against tetanus?
Ik wil graag dat u over … dagen terugkomt.	I want you to come and see me in … days' time.

PATIENT

Part 3—Nervous tension

I'm in a nervous state.	**Ik ben erg nerveus.**	ik gehn ehrkh nehr**vurss**
I'm feeling depressed.	**Ik ben erg neerslachtig.**	ik behn ehrkh nayr**slahkh**terkh
I want some sleeping pills.	**Ik zou wat slaap-tabletten willen hebben.**	ik zo^{ow} √aht **slaap**-taablehtern **√**illern **heh**bern
I can't sleep.	**Ik kan niet slapen.**	ik kahn neet **slaa**pern
I'm having nightmares.	**Ik heb last van nachtmerries.**	ik hehp lahst vahn **nahkht**-mehreess
Can you prescribe a/an ...?	**Kunt u mij ... voor-schrijven?**	kurnt ew maiy ... **voar**-skhraiyvern
anti-depressant	**een anti-depressivum**	ayn ahntee-day**prehs**seevurm
sedative	**een kalmerend middel**	ayn kahl**may**rernt **mid**derl
tranquillizer	**een rustgevend middel**	ayn **rurst**ghayvernt midderl

---

DOCTOR

3—Nervositeit

U bent overspannen.	You're suffering from nervous tension.
U hebt rust nodig.	You need a rest.
Welke tabletten hebt u tot nu toe ingenomen?	What pills have you been taking?
Hoeveel per dag?	How many a day?
Sinds wanneer voelt u zich zo?	How long have you been feeling like this?
Ik zal u wat pillen voor-schrijven.	I'll prescribe some pills.
Ik zal u een kalmerend middel geven.	I'll give you a sedative.

PATIENT

Prescriptions and dosage

What kind of medicine is this?	**Wat zijn dit voor medicijnen?**	vaht zaiyn dit voar maydee**saiy**nern
How many times a day should I take it?	**Hoeveel keer per dag moet ik ze innemen?**	hoo**vayl** kayr pehr dahkh moot ik zer **inn**aymern
Must I swallow them whole?	**Moet ik ze heel doorslikken?**	moot ik zer hayl **doar**-slikkern

Fee

How much do I owe you?	**Hoeveel ben ik u verschuldigd?**	hoo**vayl** behn ik ew vehr**skhurl**derkh
Do I pay you now or will you send me your bill?	**Zal ik nu betalen of stuurt u mij de rekening?**	zahl ik noo ber**taa**lern of stewrt ew maiy der **ray**kerning
Can you give a receipt for my health insurance?	**Kunt u mij een kwitantie geven voor mijn ziektever-zekering?**	kurnt ew maiy ayn kvee-**tahnt**see **ghay**vern voar maiyn **zeek**terverrzaykerring

---

DOCTOR

Recepten en dosering

Neemt u om de ... uur ... theelepels van deze medicijn.	Take ... teaspoons of this medicine every ... hours.
Neemt u ... ... tabletten met een glas water ...	Take ... pills with a glass of water ...
... maal per dag	... times a day
voor iedere maaltijd	before each meal
na iedere maaltijd	after each meal
's morgens	in the morning
's avonds	at night

Honorarium

Ik heb liever dat u meteen betaalt.	Please pay me now.
Ik stuur u de rekening.	I'll send you the bill.

FOR NUMBERS, see page 175

Dentist

Can you recommend a good dentist?	**Kunt u mij een goede tandarts aanbevelen?**	kurnt ew maiy ayn **ghoo**der **tahn**tahrts **aan**bervaylern
Can I make an (urgent) appointment to see Dr ...?	**Kan ik een afspraak met Dr ... maken? (Het is dringend.)**	kahn ik ayn **ahf**spraak meht **dok**terr ... **maa**kern (heht iss **dring**ernt)
Can't you possibly make it earlier than that?	**Kan het werkelijk niet eerder?**	kahn heht **ꝟehr**kerlerk neet **ayr**derr
I've a toothache.	**Ik heb kiespijn.**	ik hehp **kees**paiyn
I've an abscess.	**Ik heb een abces.**	ik hehp ayn ahp**sehss**
This tooth hurts.	**Deze tand doet pijn.**	dayzer tahnt doot paiyn
at the top	**bovenaan**	**boa**vernaan
at the bottom	**onderaan**	**on**derraan
in the front	**voorin**	**voa**rin
at the back	**achterin**	**ahkh**terrin
Can you fix it temporarily?	**Kunt u er een noodvulling in doen?**	kurnt ew ehr ayn **noat**vurling in doon
Could you give me an anaesthetic?	**Kunt u het verdoven?**	kurnt ew heht verr**doa**vern
I don't want it extracted.	**Ik wil hem niet laten trekken.**	ik ꝟil hehm neet **laa**tern **treh**kern
I've lost a filling.	**Ik heb een vulling verloren.**	ik hehp ayn **vur**ling verr**loa**rern
The gum is...	**Het tandvlees...**	heht **tahnt**vlayss
bleeding	**bloedt**	bloot
very sore	**is zeer pijnlijk**	iss zayr **paiyn**lerk

Dentures

I've broken my denture.	**Ik heb mijn gebit gebroken.**	ik hehp maiyn gher**bit** gher**broa**kern
Can you repair this denture?	**Kunt u dit gebit repareren?**	kurnt ew dit gher**bit** raypaa**ray**rern
When will it be ready?	**Wanneer is het klaar?**	ꝟah**nayr** iss heht klaar

Optician

I've broken my glasses.	**Mijn bril is gebroken.**	maiyn bril iss gher**broa**kern
Can you repair them for me?	**Kunt u het voor me repareren?**	kurnt ew heht voar mer raypaa**ray**rern
When will they be ready?	**Wanneer is het klaar?**	**∀ahnayr** iss heht klaar
Can you change the lenses?	**Kunt u er andere glazen inzetten?**	kurnt ew ehr **ahn**derrer **ghlaa**zern **in**zehtern
I want tinted lenses.	**Ik wil graag gekleurde glazen.**	ik ∀il ghraakh gher**klurr**der **ghlaa**zern
I'd like a spectacle case.	**Ik wil graag een brillekoker.**	ik ∀il ghraakh ayn **bril**lerkoakerr
I'd like to have my eyesight checked.	**Kunt u mijn gezichtsscherpte opmeten?**	kurnt ew maiyn gher**zikhts**skhehrpter **op**maytern
I've lost one of my contact lenses.	**Ik heb een van mijn contactlenzen verloren.**	ik hehp ayn vahn maiyn kon**tahkt**lehnzern verr**loa**rern
Could you give me another one?	**Kunt u mij een andere bezorgen?**	kurnt ew maiy ayn **ahn**derrer ber**zor**ghern
I have hard/soft lenses.	**Ik heb harde/zachte contactlenzen.**	ik hehp **hahr**der/**zahkh**ter kon**takt**lehnzern
Have you any contact-lens liquid?	**Hebt u contact-lenzen-vloeistof?**	hehpt ew kon**tahkt**lehnzern **vloo••**stof
A large/small bottle, please.	**Een kleine/grote fles, alstublieft.**	ayn **klaiy**ner/**ghroa**ter flehss ahlstew**bleeft**
I'd like to buy a pair of sunglasses	**Ik wil graag een zonnebril kopen.**	ik ∀il ghraakh ayn **zon**ner-bril **koa**pern
May I look in a mirror?	**Mag ik even in de spiegel kijken?**	mahkh ik **ay**vern in der **spee**gherl **kaiy**kern
I'd like to buy a pair of binoculars.	**Ik wil graag een veldkijker kopen.**	ik ∀il ghraakh ayn **vehlt**kaiykerr **koa**pern
How much do I owe you?	**Hoeveel ben ik u schuldig?**	hoo**vayl** behn ik ew **skhurl**derkh

FOR NUMBERS, see page 175

Reference section

Where do you come from?

Africa	**Afrika**	aa**free**kaa
Asia	**Azië**	aa**zee**yer
Australia	**Australië**	oas**traa**leeyer
Europe	**Europa**	ur**roa**paa
North America	**Noord-Amerika**	noart aa**may**reekaa
South America	**Zuid-Amerika**	zur^{ew}t aa**may**reekaa
Austria	**Oostenrijk**	**oa**sternraiyk
Belgium	**België**	**behl**gheeyer
Canada	**Canada**	**kah**naadaa
Denmark	**Denemarken**	**day**nermahrkern
East Germany	**Oost-Duitsland**	oast **dur^{ew}ts**lahnt
England	**Engeland**	**ehn**gerlahnt
Finland	**Finland**	**fin**lahnt
France	**Frankrijk**	**frahnk**raiyk
Great Britain	**Groot-Brittannië**	ghroat-brit**tah**neeyer
Greece	**Griekenland**	**ghree**kernlahnt
India	**India**	**in**deeyaa
Ireland	**Ierland**	**eer**lahnt
Israel	**Israël**	**is**raaehl
Italy	**Italië**	ee**taa**leeyer
Japan	**Japan**	yaa**pahn**
Luxembourg	**Luxemburg**	**lewk**sermburrkh
Morocco	**Marokko**	maa**rok**koa
Netherlands	**Nederland**	**nay**derrlahnt
New Zealand	**Nieuw-Zeeland**	nee^{oo} **zay**lahnt
Norway	**Noorwegen**	**noar**Ʋayghern
Portugal	**Portugal**	**por**tewghahl
Scotland	**Schotland**	**skhot**lahnt
South Africa	**Zuid-Afrika**	zur^{ew}t **aa**freekaa
Soviet Union	**Sowjet-Unie**	**sof**yeht **ew**nee
Spain	**Spanje**	**spah**nyer
Sweden	**Zweden**	**zƲay**dern
Switzerland	**Zwitserland**	**zƲit**serrlahnt
Tunisia	**Tunesië**	tew**nay**seeyer
Turkey	**Turkije**	turr**kai**yyer
United States	**Verenigde Staten**	vehraynerghder **staa**tern
Wales	**Wales**	**Ʋay**lerss
West Germany	**West-Duitsland**	Ʋehst **dur^{ew}ts**lahnt
Yugoslavia	**Joegoslavië**	yoogho**slaa**veeyer

Numbers

0	**nul**	nurl
1	**een**	ayn
2	**twee**	t∀ay
3	**drie**	dree
4	**vier**	veer
5	**vijf**	vaiyf
6	**zes**	zehss
7	**zeven**	zayvern
8	**acht**	ahkht
9	**negen**	nayghern
10	**tien**	teen
11	**elf**	ehlf
12	**twaalf**	t∀aalf
13	**dertien**	dehrteen
14	**veertien**	vayrteen
15	**vijftien**	vaiyfteen
16	**zestien**	zehsteen
17	**zeventien**	zayvernteen
18	**achttien**	ahkhteen
19	**negentien**	nayghernteen
20	**twintig**	t∀interkh
21	**eenentwintig**	aynernt∀inerkh
22	**tweeëntwintig**	t∀ayyernt∀interkh
23	**drieëntwintig**	dreeyernt∀interkh
24	**vierentwintig**	veerernt∀interkh
25	**vijfentwintig**	vaiyfernt∀interkh
26	**zesentwintig**	zehsernt∀interkh
27	**zevenentwintig**	zayvernernt∀interkh
28	**achtentwintig**	ahkhternt∀interkh
29	**negenentwintig**	naynghernernt∀interkh
30	**dertig**	dehrterkh
31	**eenendertig**	aynerndehrterkh
32	**tweeëndertig**	t∀ayyerndehrterkh
33	**drieëndertig**	dreeyerndehrterkh
40	**veertig**	vayrterkh
41	**eenenveertig**	aynernvayrterkh
42	**tweeënveertig**	t∀ayyernvayrterkh
43	**drieënveertig**	dreeyernvayrterkh
50	**vijftig**	vaiyfterkh
51	**eenenvijftig**	aynernvaiyfterkh
52	**tweeënvijftig**	t∀ayyernvaiyfterkh
53	**drieënvijftig**	dreeyernvaiyfterkh
60	**zestig**	zehsterkh
61	**eenenzestig**	aynernsehsterkh

REFERENCE SECTION

62	**tweeënzestig**	**tꝟay**yernsehsterkh
63	**drieënzestig**	**dree**yernsehsterkh
70	**zeventig**	**zay**vernterkh
71	**eenenzeventig**	**ay**nernsayvernterkh
72	**tweeënzeventig**	**tꝟay**yernsayvernterkh
73	**drieënzeventig**	**dree**yernsayvernterkh
80	**tachtig**	**tahkh**terkh
81	**eenentachtig**	**ay**nerntahkhterkh
82	**tweeëntachtig**	**tꝟay**yerntahkhterkh
83	**drieëntachtig**	**dree**yerntahkhterkh
90	**negentig**	**nay**ghernterkh
91	**eenennegentig**	**ay**nernnayghernterkh
92	**tweeënnegentig**	**tꝟay**yernnayghernterkh
93	**drieënnegentig**	**dree**yernnayghernterkh
100	**honderd**	**hon**derrt
101	**honderd één**	**hon**derrt ayn
102	**honderd twee**	**hon**derrt tꝟay
110	**honderd tien**	**hon**derrt teen
120	**honderd twintig**	**hon**derrt **tꝟin**terkh
130	**honderd dertig**	**hon**derrt **dehr**terkh
140	**honderd veertig**	**hon**derrt **vayr**terkh
150	**honderd vijftig**	**hon**derrt **vaiyf**terkh
160	**honderd zestig**	**hon**derrt **sehs**terkh
170	**honderd zeventig**	**hon**derrt **say**vernterkh
180	**honderd tachtig**	**hon**derrt **tahkh**terkh
190	**honderd negentig**	**hon**derrt **nay**ghernterkh
200	**tweehonderd**	**tꝟay**honderrt
300	**driehonderd**	**dree**honderrt
400	**vierhonderd**	**veer**honderrt
500	**vijfhonderd**	**vaiyf**honderrt
600	**zeshonderd**	**zehs**honderrt
700	**zevenhonderd**	**zay**vernhonderrt
800	**achthonderd**	**ahkht**honderrt
900	**negenhonderd**	**nay**ghernhonderrt
1000	**duizend**	**dur^{ew}**zernt
1100	**elfhonderd**	**ehlf**honderrt
1200	**twaalfhonderd**	**tꝟaalf**honderrt
2000	**tweeduizend**	**tꝟay**dur^{ew}zernt
5000	**vijfduizend**	**vaiyf**dur^{ew}zernt
10,000	**tienduizend**	**teen**dur^{ew}zernt
50,000	**vijftigduizend**	**vaiyf**terghdur^{ew}zernt
100,000	**honderdduizend**	**hon**derrtdur^{ew}zernt
1,000,000	**een miljoen**	ayn mil**yoon**
1,000,000,000	**een miljard**	ayn mil**yahrt**

first	**eerste**	ayrster
second	**tweede**	**t∀ay**der
third	**derde**	**dehr**der
fourth	**vierde**	**veer**der
fifth	**vijfde**	**vaiyf**der
sixth	**zesde**	**zehs**der
seventh	**zevende**	**zay**verder
eighth	**achtste**	**ahkt**ster
ninth	**negende**	**nay**ghernder
tenth	**tiende**	**teen**der
once	**eenmaal**	**ayn**maal
twice	**tweemaal**	**t∀ay**maal
three times	**driemaal**	**dree**maal
a half	**een helft**	ayn hehlft
half a...	**een halve...**	ayn **hahl**ver
half of...	**de helft van**	der hehlft vahn
half (adj.)	**half, halve**	hahlf **hahl**ver
a quarter	**een kwart**	ayn k∀ahrt
one third	**een derde**	ayn **dehr**der
a pair of	**een paar...**	ayn paar ...
a dozen	**een dozijn...**	ayn doa**zaiyn**
I'm 26 years old.	**Ik ben 26.**	ik behn 26
He was born in 1940.	**Hij is in 1940 geboren.**	haiy iss in 1940 gher**boa**rern
1985	**negentien vijf-ëntachtig**	**nay**ghernteen **vaiy**ferntahkhterkh
1987	**negentien zeven-ëntachtig**	**nay**ghernteen **zay**vernerntahkhterkh
1990	**negentien negentig**	**nay**ghernteen **nay**ghernterkh

Time

Het is kwart over twaalf. ('s middags)*
(heht iss k∀ahrt oaverr t∀aalf [smiddahkhs])

Het is tien voor half twee.
(heht iss teen voar hahlf t∀ay)

Het is half vier.
(heht iss hahlf veer)

Het is vijf over half vijf.
(heht iss vaiyf oaverr hahlf vaiyf)

Het is kwart voor zeven.
(heht iss k∀ahrt voar zayvern)

Het is tien voor acht.
(heht iss teen voar ahkht)

Het is tien uur.
(heht iss teen ewr)

Het is vijf over elf.
(heht iss vaiyf oaverr ehlf)

Het is tien over twaalf. ('s nachts)**
(heht iss teen oaverr t∀aalf [snahkhts])

* = 12.15 p.m. ** = 12.10 a.m.

Note: In ordinary conversation, time is expressed as shown here. However, official time uses the 24-hour clock. For instance, 13.15 corresponds to 1.15 p.m. and 20.30 to 8.30. At midnight, time returns to 0 so that 12.17 a.m. is written 0.17.

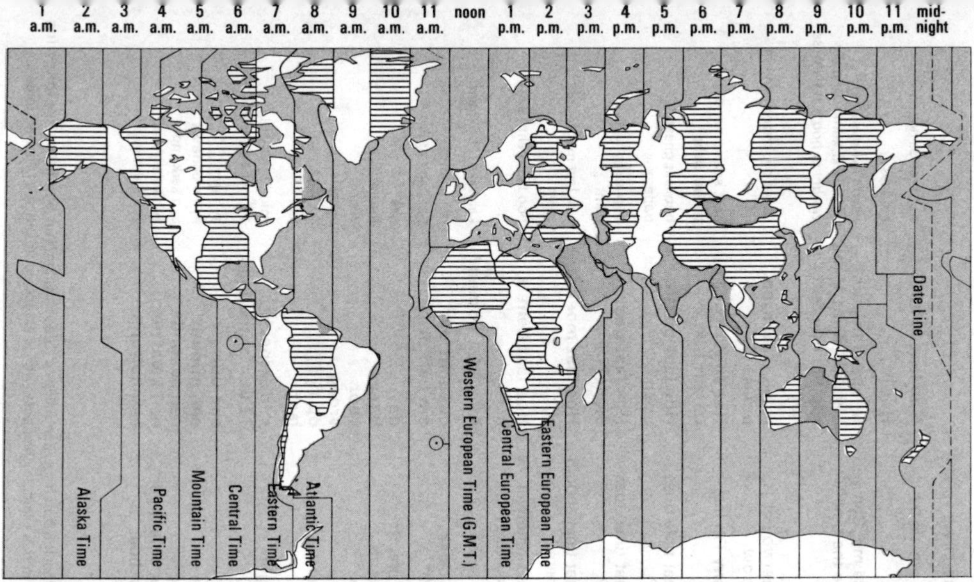

Countries which have adopted a time differing from that in the corresponding time zone. Note that also in the USSR, official time is one hour ahead of the time in each corresponding time zone. In summer, numerous countries advance time one hour ahead of standard time.

What time is it?

What time is it?	**Hoe laat is het?**	hoo laat iss heht
It's ...	**Het is ...**	heht iss
Excuse me. Can you tell me the time?	**Neemt u mij niet kwalijk. Kunt U mij zeggen hoe laat het is?**	naymt ew maiy neet k**√aa**lerk. kurnt ew maiy **zeh**ghern hoo laat heht iss
I'll meet you at ... tomorrow.	**Ik zie u morgen om ...**	ik zee ew **mor**ghern om
I'm sorry I'm late.	**Het spijt me dat ik te laat ben.**	heht spaiyt mer daht ik ter laat behn
At what time does ... open?	**Hoe laat gaat ... open?**	hoo laat ghaat ... **oa**pern
At what time does ... close?	**Hoe laat gaat ... dicht?**	hoo laat ghaat ... dikht
At what time should I be there?	**Hoe laat moet ik er zijn?**	hoo laat moot ik ehr zaiyn
At what time will you be there?	**Hoe laat bent u er?**	hoo laat behnt ew ehr
Can I come ...?	**Kan ik ... komen?**	kahn ik ... **koa**mern
at 8 o'clock	**om acht uur**	om ahkht ewr
at 2.30*	**om half drie***	om hahlf dree
after (prep.)	**na**	naa
afterwards	**later**	**laa**terr
before	**voor**	voar
early	**vroeg**	vrookh
in time	**op tijd**	op taiyt
late	**laat**	laat
midnight	**middernacht**	**mid**derrnahkht
noon	**12 uur 's middags**	12 ewr s**mid**dahkhs
hour	**een uur**	ayn ewr
minute	**een minuut**	ayn mee**newt**
second	**een seconde**	ayn ser**kon**der
quarter of an hour	**een kwartier**	ayn k√ahr**teer**
half an hour	**een half uur**	ayn hahlf ewr

* Note that the Dutch say, not "half past" the preceding hour, but "half to" the **following** hour; in this example "half past two" is expressed in Dutch as "half to three".

REFERENCE SECTION

Days

What day is it today?	**Welke dag is het vandaag?**	**Ꝟehl**ker dahkh iss heht vahn**daakh**
Sunday	**zondag**	**zon**dahkh
Monday	**maandag**	**maan**dahkh
Tuesday	**dinsdag**	**dins**dahkh
Wednesday	**woensdag**	**Ꝟoons**dahkh
Thursday	**donderdag**	**donderr**dahkh
Friday	**vrijdag**	**vraiy**dahkh
Saturday	**zaterdag**	**zaaterr**dahkh
in the morning	**'s morgens**	**smor**ghernss
during the day	**overdag**	oaverr**dahkh**
in the afternoon	**'s middags**	**smid**dahkhs
in the evening	**'s avonds**	**saa**vonts
at night	**'s nachts**	snahkhts
the day before yesterday	**eergisteren**	ayr**ghis**terrern
yesterday	**gisteren**	**ghis**terrern
today	**vandaag**	vahn**daakh**
tomorrow	**morgen**	**mor**ghern
the day after tomorrow	**overmorgen**	**oa**verrmorghern
the day before	**de vorige dag**	der **voa**rergher dahkh
the next day	**de volgende dag**	der **vol**ghernder dahkh
two days ago	**twee dagen geleden**	tꝟay **daa**ghern gher**lay**dern
in three days' time	**over drie dagen**	**oa**verr dree **daa**ghern
last week	**verleden week**	verr**lay**dern ꝟayk
next week	**volgende week**	**vol**ghernder ꝟayk
for a fortnight (two weeks)	**gedurende twee weken**	gher**dew**rernder tꝟay **ꝟay**kern
birthday	**de verjaardag**	der verr**yaar**dahkh
day	**de dag**	der dahkh
day off	**de vrije dag**	der **vrai**yyer dahkh
holiday	**de feestdag**	der **fayst**dahkh
holidays	**de vakantie**	der vaa**kahnt**see
month	**de maand**	der maant
vacation	**de vakantie**	der vaa**kahnt**see
week	**de week**	der ꝟayk
weekday	**de weekdag**	der **ꝟayk**dahkh
weekend	**het weekeinde**	heht **ꝟayk**aiynder
working day	**de werkdag**	der **ꝟehrk**dahkh

Months

January	**januari**	yahnewaaree
February	**februari**	faybrewaaree
March	**maart**	maart
April	**april**	aapril
May	**mei**	maiy
June	**juni**	yewnee
July	**juli**	yewlee
August	**augustus**	o^{ow}ghursturss
September	**september**	sehptehmberr
October	**oktober**	oktoaberr
November	**november**	noavehmberr
December	**december**	daysehmberr
since June	**sinds juni**	sints yewnee
during the month of August	**tijdens de maand augustus**	taiydernss der maant o^{ow}ghursturss
last month	**de vorige maand**	der voarergher maant
next month	**de volgende maand**	der volghernder maant
the month before	**de maand daarvoor**	der maant daarvoar
the next month	**de maand daarop**	der maant daarop
July 1	**1 juli**	ayn yewlee
March 17	**17 maart**	zayvernteen maart

Note: The names of days and months are not capitalized in Dutch.

Letter headings are written thus:

Amsterdam, August 17, 19..	**Amsterdam, 17 augustus 19..**
Utrecht, July 1, 19..	**Utrecht, 1 juli 19..**

Seasons

spring	**de lente**	der lehnter
summer	**de zomer**	der zoamerr
autumn	**de herfst**	der hehrfst
winter	**de winter**	der Vinterr
in spring	**in de lente**	in der lehnter
during the summer	**in de zomer/ 's zomers**	in der zoamerr/soamerrss
in autumn	**in de herfst**	in der hehrfst
during the winter	**in de winter/ 's winters**	in der Vinterr/sVinterrss

Public holidays

Listed below you'll find the dates of national holidays *(openbare feestdag)* celebrated in Holland (NL) and Belgium (B).

January 1	**Nieuwjaarsdag**	New Years's Day	NL	B
April 30	**Koninginnedag**	Queen's Birthday	NL	
May 1	**Dag van de Arbeid**	Labour Day		B
May 5	**Bevrijdingsdag**	Liberation Day (once every 5 years: 1980, 1985 etc.)	NL	
July 21	**Nationale Feestdag**	National Day		B
August 15	**Maria Hemelvaart**	Assumption Day		B
November 11	**Wapenstilstandsdag**	Armistice Day		B
December 25 and 26	**Kerstfeest**	Christmas and St. Stephen's Days	NL	B
Movable dates:	**Goede Vrijdag**	Good Friday	NL	
	Paasmaandag	Easter Monday	NL	B
	Hemelvaartsdag	Ascension Thursday	NL	B
	Pinkstermaandag	Whit Monday	NL	B

The year round

The climate in Holland and Belgium is quite unpredictable! Summer days may be either rainy and chilly or gloriously hot and dry. Mild—even warm—spells in spring and autumn are by no means uncommon, and winters are more often rainy and grey than outright cold. Real freeze-ups are rare.

		J	F	M	A	M	J	J	A	S	O	N	D
Amsterdam	F	39	39	42	51	57	61	67	65	57	51	42	39
	C	4	4	6	11	14	16	19	18	14	11	6	4
Days with no rain		12	13	18	16	19	18	17	17	15	13	11	12
Brussels	F	36	36	41	44	51	60	62	63	59	51	41	37
	C	2	2	5	7	11	16	17	17	15	11	5	3
Days with no rain		19	18	20	18	21	19	20	20	19	19	18	18

Common abbreviations

afz.	**afzender**	from…
A.N.W.B.	**Wegenwacht**	Dutch Touring Club
a.s.	**aanstaande**	next
a.u.b.	**alstublieft**	please
a/z	**aan zee**	on sea
blz.	**bladzijde**	page
B.T.W.	**Belasting Toegevoegde Waarde**	value added tax (VAT)
b.v.	**bijvoorbeeld**	for example
CS	**Centraal Station**	Central Station
Dhr.	**de heer**	Mr. (written)
d.w.z.	**dat wil zeggen**	i.e.
E.H.B.O.	**Eerste Hulp bij Ongelukken**	first-aid organization
enz.	**enzovoort**	etc.
excl.	**exclusief**	not included
G.G.D.	**Gemeentelijke Geneeskundige Dienst**	local ambulance service
GWK-bank	**grenswisselkantoren**	frontier exchange offices
inl.	**inlichtingen**	information
j.l.	**jongstleden**	last
K.A.C.B.	**Koninklijke Automobiel Club van België**	Royal Belgian Automobile Club
K.N.A.C.	**Koninklijke Nederlandse Automobiel Club**	Royal Dutch Automobile Club
m.	**mijnheer**	Mr. (spoken)
mej.	**mejuffrouw**	Miss
mevr. (mw.)	**mevrouw**	Mrs.
N.J.H.C.	**Stichting Nederlandse Jeugdherberg Centrale**	Dutch Youth Hostels Organization
NL	**Nederland**	Netherlands
n.m.	**namiddag**	a.m.
no.	**nummer**	number
p.a. or p/a	**per adres**	care of
r.-k.	**rooms-katholiek**	Roman Catholic
v.m.	**voormiddag**	p.m.
z.o.z.	**zie ommezijde**	please turn page

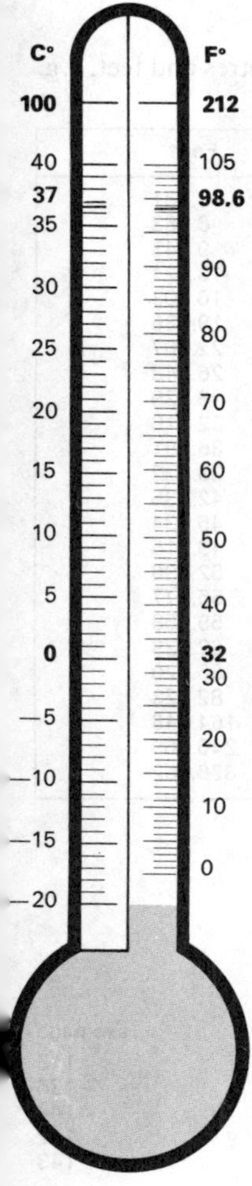

Conversion tables

Centimetres and inches

To change centimetres into inches, multiply by .39.

To change inches into centimetres, multiply by 2.54.

	in.	feet	yards
1 mm	0.039	0.003	0.001
1 cm	0.39	0.03	0.01
1 dm	3.94	0.32	0.10
1 m	39.40	3.28	1.09

	mm	cm	m
1 in.	25.4	2.54	0.025
1 ft.	304.8	30.48	0.304
1 yd.	914.4	91.44	0.914

(32 metres = 35 yards)

Temperature

To convert Centigrade into degrees Fahrenheit, multiply Centigrade by 1.8 and add 32.

To convert degrees Fahrenheit into Centigrade, subtract 32 from Fahrenheit and divide by 1.8.

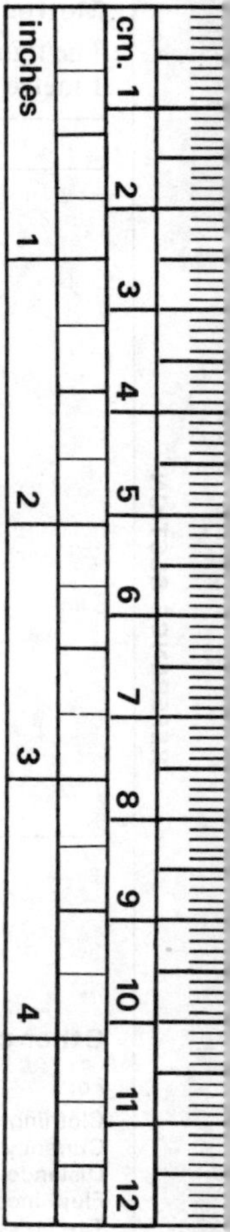

Metres and feet

The figure in the middle stands for both metres and feet, e.g. 1 metre = 3.28 ft. and 1 foot = 0.30 m.

Metres		Feet
0.30	**1**	3.281
0.61	**2**	6.563
0.91	**3**	9.843
1.22	**4**	13.124
1.52	**5**	16.403
1.83	**6**	19.686
2.13	**7**	22.967
2.44	**8**	26.248
2.74	**9**	29.529
3.05	**10**	32.810
3.35	**11**	36.091
3.66	**12**	39.372
3.96	**13**	42.635
4.27	**14**	45.934
4.57	**15**	49.215
4.88	**16**	52.496
5.18	**17**	55.777
5.49	**18**	59.058
5.79	**19**	62.339
6.10	**20**	65.620
7.62	**25**	82.023
15.24	**50**	164.046
22.86	**75**	246.069
30.48	**100**	328.092

Other conversion charts

Weight conversion

The figure in the middle stands for both kilograms and pounds, e.g., 1 kilogram = 2.205 lb. and 1 pound = 0.45 kilograms.

Kilograms (kg.)		Avoirdupois pounds
0.45	1	2.205
0.90	2	4.405
1.35	3	6.614
1.80	4	8.818
2.25	5	11.023
2.70	6	13.227
3.15	7	15.432
3.60	8	17.636
4.05	9	19.840
4.50	10	22.045
6.75	15	33.068
9.00	20	44.889
11.25	25	55.113
22.50	50	110.225
33.75	75	165.338
45.00	100	220.450

NOORD
(noart)
NORTH

WEST
(vehst)
WEST

OOST
(oast)
EAST

ZUID
(zur^{ew}t)
SOUTH

What does that sign mean?

You're sure to encounter some of these signs or notices on your trip.

Bellen, a.u.b.	Please ring
Bezet	Occupied
Dames	Ladies
Deur sluiten	Close the door
Duwen	Push
Eerst kloppen	Knock before entering
Geopend van ... tot ...	Open from ... to ...
Gereserveerd	Reserved
Gesloten	Closed
Heet	Hot
Heren	Gentlemen
Hoogspanning	High voltage
Ingang	Entrance
Inlichtingen	Information
Kassa	Cashier's (cash desk)
Koud	Cold
Levensgevaar	Danger of death
Lift	Lift (elevator)
Mannen	Men
Niet aanraken, a.u.b.	Do not touch
Niet roken	No smoking
Nooduitgang	Emergency exit
Open	Open
Opgepast	Caution
Pas op voor de hond	Beware of the dog
Privé	Private
Privéweg	Private road
Rijwielpad (fietspad)	Cycle path
Roken	Smoking
Roken verboden	No smoking
Te huur	To let (for hire)
Te koop	For sale
Trekken	Pull
Uitgang	Exit
Uitverkoop	Sales
Verboden toegang	No entrance
Voetgangers	Pedestrians
Voor honden verboden	Dogs not allowed
Vrij	Vacant
Vrije toegang	Admission free
's Zondags gesloten	Closed on Sundays

REFERENCE SECTION

Emergency

Emergency telephone numbers for fire (*brandweer*—**brahnt**∀ayr), accidents (*ongevallen*—**on**ghervahllern) and police (*politie*—poa**leet**see) vary from place to place. For large cities which have their own telephone books, these are given on the outside back cover of the publication. In the case of smaller towns and villages which are comprised within a regional telephone book, the emergency numbers are listed immediately after the locality heading.

Be quick	**Snel**	snehl
Call the police	**Roep de politie**	roop der poa**leet**see
CAREFUL	**VOORZICHTIG**	voar**zikh**terkh
Come here	**Kom hier**	kom heer
Come in	**Binnen**	**bin**nern
Danger	**Gevaar**	gher**vaar**
FIRE	**BRAND**	brahnt
Gas	**Gas**	ghahss
GET A DOCTOR	**ROEP EEN DOKTER**	roop ayn **dok**terr
Get help quickly	**Haal snel hulp**	haal snehl hurlp
Go away	**Ga weg**	ghaa ∀ehkh
HELP	**HELP**	hehlp
I'm ill	**Ik ben ziek**	ik behn zeek
I'm lost	**Ik ben verdwaald**	ik behn verr**d∀alt**
I've lost my…	**Ik heb … mijn verloren**	ik hehp maiyn … verr**loa**rern
Keep your hands to yourself	**Handen thuis**	**hahn**dern tur^{ew}ss
Leave me alone	**Laat me met rust**	laat mer meht rurst
Lie down	**Ga liggen**	ghaa **li**ghern
Listen	**Luister**	**lur^{ew}**sterr
Listen to me	**Luister naar mij**	**lur^{ew}**sterr naar maiy
Look	**Kijk**	kaiyk
Look out	**Pas op**	pahss op
POLICE	**POLITIE**	poa**leet**see
Quick	**Vlug**	vlurkh
STOP	**STOP**	stop
Stop here	**Hier stoppen**	heer **stop**pern
Stop or I'll scream	**Houd op of ik gil**	ho^{ow} op of ik ghil
Stop that man	**Houd die man tegen**	ho^{ow} dee mahn **tay**ghern
STOP THIEF	**HOUD DE DIEF**	ho^{ow} der deef
Wait a minute	**Een ogenblik**	ayn **oa**ghernblik

FOR CAR ACCIDENTS, see page 150

Index

Quick reference page

Please.	**Alstublieft.**	ahlstew**bleeft**
Thank you.	**Dank u wel.**	dahnk ew ∀ehl
Yes/No.	**Ja/Nee.**	yaa/nay
Excuse me.	**Neemt u mij niet kwalijk.**	naymt ew maiy neet k∀**aa**lerk
Waiter, please!	**Ober!**	**oa**berr
How much is that?	**Hoeveel kost het?**	hoo**vayl** kost heht
Where are the toilets?	**Waar zijn de toiletten?**	∀aar zaiyn der t∀aa**leh**tern

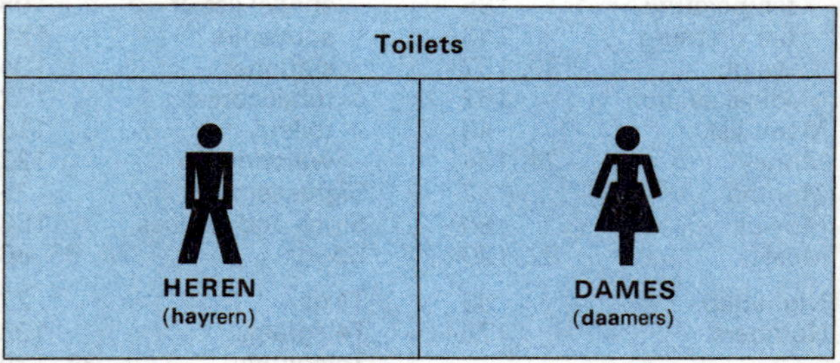

Could you tell me...?	**Kunt u mij zeggen...?**	kurnt ew maiy **zeh**ghern
where/when/why	**waar/wanneer/ waarom**	∀aar/∀ah**nayr**/∀aa**rom**
What time is it?	**Hoe laat is het?**	hoo laat iss heht
Help me, please.	**Help mij, alstublieft.**	hehlp maiy ahlstew**bleeft**
Where is the ... consulate?	**Waar is het ... consulaat?**	∀aar iss heht ... konsew**laat**
American	**Amerikaanse**	aamayree**kaan**sser
British	**Engelse**	**ehng**erlsser
Canadian	**Canadese**	kahnaa**day**sser
What does this mean?	**Wat betekent dit?**	∀aht ber**tay**kernt dit
I don't understand.	**Ik begrijp het niet.**	ik ber**graiyp** heht neet
Do you speak English?	**Spreekt u Engels?**	spraykt ew **ehng**erlss

Say BERLITZ®

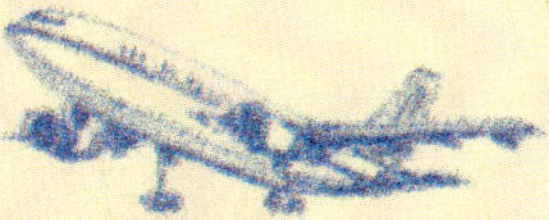

... and most people think of outstanding language schools. But Berlitz has also become the world's leading publisher of books for travellers – Travel Guides, Phrase Books, Dictionaries – plus Cassettes and Self-teaching courses.

Informative, accurate, up-to-date, Books from Berlitz are written with freshness and style. They also slip easily into pocket or purse – no need for bulky, old-fashioned volumes.

Join the millions who know how to travel. Whether for fun or business, put Berlitz in your pocket.

BERLITZ®

Leader in
Books and Cassettes
for Travellers

A division of Macmillan, Inc.

BERLITZ® Books for travellers

TRAVEL GUIDES

They fit your pocket in both size and price. Modern, up-to-date, Berlitz gets all the information you need into 128 lively pages with colour maps and photos throughout. What to see and do, where to shop, what to eat and drink, how to save.

AFRICA	Kenya Morocco South Africa Tunisia
ASIA, MIDDLE EAST	China (256 pages) Hong Kong India (256 pages) Japan (256 pages) Singapore Sri Lanka Thailand Egypt Jerusalem and the Holy Land Saudi Arabia
AUSTRAL-ASIA	Australia (256 pages)* New Zealand
BRITISH ISLES	Channel Islands London Ireland Oxford and Stratford Scotland
BELGIUM	Brussels

*in preparation

PHRASE BOOKS

World's bestselling phrase books feature all the expressions and vocabulary you'll need, and pronunciation throughout. 192 pages, 2 colours.

Arabic
Chinese
Danish
Dutch
Finnish
French
German
Greek
Hebrew
Hungarian
Italian
Japanese
Norwegian
Polish
Portuguese
Russian
Serbo-Croatian
Spanish (Castilian)
Spanish (Lat. Am.)
Swahili
Swedish
Turkish
European Phrase Book
European Menu Reader

FRANCE	Brittany France (256 pages) French Riviera Loire Valley Normandy* Paris
GERMANY	Berlin Munich The Rhine Valley
AUSTRIA and SWITZER-LAND	Tyrol Vienna Switzerland (192 pages)
GREECE, CYPRUS & TURKEY	Athens Corfu Crete Rhodes Greek Islands of the Aegean Peloponnese Salonica and Northern Greece Cyprus Istanbul/Aegean Coast
ITALY and MALTA	Florence Italian Adriatic Italian Riviera Italy (256 pages)* Rome Sicily Venice Malta
NETHER-LANDS and SCANDI-NAVIA	Amsterdam Copenhagen Helsinki Oslo and Bergen Stockholm
PORTUGAL	Algarve Lisbon Madeira
SPAIN	Barcelona and Costa Dorada Canary Islands Costa Blanca Costa Brava Costa del Sol and Andalusia Ibiza and Formentera Madrid Majorca and Minorca
EASTERN EUROPE	Budapest Dubrovnik and Southern Dalmatia Hungary (192 pages) Istria and Croatian Coast Moscow & Leningrad Split and Dalmatia
NORTH AMERICA	U.S.A. (256 pages) California Florida Hawaii New York Toronto Montreal
CARIBBEAN, LATIN AMERICA	Puerto Rico Virgin Islands Bahamas Bermuda French West Indies Jamaica Southern Caribbean Mexico City Rio de Janeiro
EUROPE	Business Travel Guide – Europe (368 pages) Pocket guide to Europe (480 pages) Cities of Europe (504 pages)
CRUISE GUIDES	Caribbean cruise guide (368 pages) Alaska cruise guide (168 pages) Handbook to Cruising (240 pages)

*in preparation

Most titles with British and U.S. destinations are available in French, German, Spanish and as many as 7 other languages.

DICTIONARIES

Bilingual with 12,500 concepts each way. Highly practical for travellers, with pronunciation shown plus menu reader, basic expressions and useful information. Over 330 pages.

Danish	Finnish	German	Norwegian	Spanish
Dutch	French	Italian	Portuguese	Swedish

Berlitz Books, a world of information in your pocket!
At all leading bookshops and airport newsstands.

Finally... a fast, fun, and affordable way to learn a foreign language...

INTRODUCING THE BERLITZ EXPRESS PROGRAMS

Self-study programs for beginners

Available in:

- Spanish
- French
- German
- Italian

Imagine, in a short time from now, being able to speak an entirely new language. French, perhaps. Or Spanish. German. Or Italian.

Berlitz, the world-renowned language instruction institution, has developed these self-study programs *expressly* for those people who want to learn to speak a foreign language *fast*. And without going through the tedious, repetitive drills and grammar rule memorization that are featured in other courses.

Instead, with the Berlitz Express programs, you learn to speak *naturally*, by listening to—and then joining in on—"real-life" dialogue on cassette tapes. This helps you *absorb* correct grammar and vocabulary almost unconsciously. And because the tapes use *sound effects* to convey meaning, you can learn your new language while you're driving, biking, walking, or doing just about anything.

Each Express Program Contains:

- TWO CASSETTES TOTALLING 100 minutes of instruction and using lively *sound effects* to identify objects, actions, and situations in your new language.
- LESSON TEXT explains new words and grammar variations as you encounter them.
- BERLITZ ROTARY VERB FINDER. How do you change the expression "I go" to "I will go" or "I went" in the language you're learning? Just spin the dial and you'll have your answer for a wide variety of common verbs.
- CONVENIENT STORAGE ALBUM protects tapes, book, and Verb Finder from damage.

Dial (no charge, USA)
24 hours, 7 days a week.

In the U.S.A.
1-800-431-9003

In Great Britain
0323-638221

Refer to Dept. No. 11604. Why not give us a ring – right now!

Treat yourself to an hour with BERLITZ®

Just listen and repeat

It's fun, not work. And you'll surprise your friends and yourself: it's so easy to pick up some basic expressions in the foreign language of your choice. These cassettes are recorded in hi-fi with four voices. Bringing native speakers into your home, they permit you to improve your accent and learn the basic phrases before you depart.

With each cassette is a helpful 32-page script, containing pronunciation tips, plus complete text of the dual-language recording.

An ideal companion for your Berlitz phrase book, pocket dictionary or travel guide. Order now!

$9.95/£5.95 (incl. VAT)

use convenient envelope attached.